IT investment
making a business case

Acknowledgement

This book has evolved over a period of many years and consequently many individuals have make a contribution to influencing the thinking and the models discussed. This has included colleagues, clients, students and a mass of literature written around the theme of information technology evaluation.

However there is one person who I would especially like to acknowledge – someone who has made an important contribution to the thinking behind this book. Dr Michael Sherwood-Smith's work, which began with his PhD dissertation at the end of the 1980s, has been very influential in directing my attention to the process issues behind information technology evaluation. As an information technology academic and consultant Dr Michael Sherwood-Smith was one of the early advocates of using a process of continuous participative evaluation, or active benefit realisation, to focus on information technology benefit identification and subsequent delivery. It was as a result of my work with him in this area during the early 1990s that some of the ideas used in this book originally sprang.

Dan Remenyi

IT investment
making a business case

Dr Dan Remenyi

OXFORD AUCKLAND BOSTON JOHANNESBURG MELBOURNE NEW DELHI

Butterworth-Heinemann
Linacre House, Jordan Hill, Oxford OX2 8DP
225 Wildwood Avenue, Woburn, MA 01801-2041
A division of Reed Educational and Professional Publishing Ltd

A member of the Reed Elsevier plc group

First published 1999
© MCIL 1999

British Library Cataloguing in Publication Data
A catalogue record for this book is available from the British Library

ISBN 0 7506 4504 0

Typeset by P.K.McBride, Southampton
Printed and bound in Great Britain

PLANT A TREE

BTCV
British Trust for
Conservation Volunteers

FOR EVERY TITLE THAT WE PUBLISH, BUTTERWORTH-HEINEMANN
WILL PAY FOR BTCV TO PLANT AND CARE FOR A TREE.

Contents

About the author

Dr Dan Remenyi has spent more than 25 years working in the field of corporate computers and information systems. He has worked with computers as an IS professional, business consultant and as a user. In all these capacities he has been primarily concerned with benefit realisation and obtaining the maximum value for money from  the organisations' information systems investment and effort. In recent years he has specialised in the area of the formulation and the implementation of strategic information systems and how to evaluate the performance of these and other systems. He has also worked extensively in the field of information systems project management, specialising in the area of project risk identification and management. He has written a number of books and papers in the field of IT management and regularly conducts courses and seminar as well as working as a consultant in this area. His most recent books published include *Achieving Maximum Value from Information Systems – A Process Approach* and *Stop IT Failure through Risk Management.*

He has worked over the years for many organisations both as a management consultant and as an executive development facilitator in different parts of the world. These organisations include FI Group, Caterpillar Division of Barlows, Andersen Consulting, National Health Service in the United Kingdom, Spoornet (the national railroad company of South Africa), Liberty Life Insurance Company, and the Anglo Vaal Mining Corporation.

Dan Remenyi holds a B.Soc.Sc., an MBA and a PhD. He is a Visiting Professor at Brunel University, Uxbridge.

E-mail: remenyi@compuserve.com

How to use this book

This is a wide-ranging book, which addresses a number of different aspects of a challenging subject. Those who are new to this subject may wish to read the book from the start while others may wish to dip into difference sections to look at particular concepts which interest them.

This book offers practical hands-on advice as to how to prepare a business case for an IT investment.

It begins with a discussion of why it is necessary to make a business case for an IT investment and goes on to look at what preparation is required within the organisation by those who will be making the business case before it can be developed.

In Chapters 1 to 3 general description is offered, of important background issues as well as the importance of using a process approach to making the business case. The process approach underpins the rest of the business case creation.

Chapters 4 to 8 address the five major components of the IT investment business case.

Chapter 9 is focused on business case accounting and looks at a number of different approaches to this issue.

Chapter 10 describes how to evaluate a business case and how to compare one business case with another.

Chapter 11 indicates how the business case may be used as a major component of IT project management.

Appendices A, B, D, E, and F contain useful forms, which may be used in implementing the framework described in the book. These forms are currently available on the World-wide Web at:

http://www.bh.com/samples

Preface

Business executives are demanding, by expressing their dissatisfaction at the way in which information systems departments or functions have been controlled, a new approach to the management of this important aspect of many organisations.

This new approach requires a new understanding of the role and function of information systems and IT investment in organisations. The emphasis is being placed on what IT investment can do to support more efficient and effective business process and practices. This current understanding of IT investment and the role and function of information systems in organisations is based on what has sometimes been called a paradigm shift, although the expression *paradigm shift* is now considered to be grossly overworked. The computer community has been arguing that information systems are of central importance to the organisation. They have claimed that information systems are a most valuable element or aspect of the range of resources available to many businesses. They have asserted that information systems expenditure should be regarded as contributing towards building a strategic asset and not an expense. In addition, the computer community has continually claimed that they have not been credited with sufficient importance in the hierarchy of the organisation. They have objected to being seen, as they sometimes are, as an extension of the finance and accounting division. They frequently assert their claim to be led by an individual who has a position on the board of directors in his or her own right as an information systems specialist.

Although none of these demands are necessarily wrong or inappropriate, they have generally led to a perception of information systems which has, in many cases, been less than useful. This perception, which is based on the importance of computers in their own right, has been a stumbling block to optimising the effective and efficient use of information systems throughout the organisation.

The way forward is to rethink and rearticulate the role, function and the locus of information systems.

It is useful to start this process of rethinking information systems management by going back to some fundamental concepts. To use classical economic language, an information system is a capital or producer good. A capital or producer good is something that is not acquired or valued for the utility it delivers by itself in its own right. Simply, capital goods do not have any intrinsic utility or value in their own right, as a television set, a jacket, a meal or a holiday in the sun does. A capital or producer good is desired because it can be used to produce other goods and services, which in turn may offer us utility and value such as the television set, a jacket, a meal or a holiday. A bulldozer is a clear example of a capital or producer good. A bulldozer has no intrinsic value on its own. In fact it could be seen as a liability as it takes up much space, is costly to move about and requires expensive maintenance. A bulldozer's value is in the result of its use, i.e. the hole in the ground, the levelling of the old building or the preparing of the ground for a new road or motorway surface.

Because information systems are also capital or producer goods their ability to be useful or deliver value operates in much the same way. An information system has no intrinsic value in its own right. By itself an information system is nothing more than a sunk cost, and normally a very large cost at that. An information system only acquires value when it is used as part of a business process or practice that will result in the enhancement of the effectiveness or the efficiency of the organisation.

Business processes or practices are made to function by people working as groups or individuals in line positions. They make, sell and support the products or services for which the organisation was created. It is these line people who know what is required by their organisations and how information systems can best support their business efforts. These groups or individuals use the information systems to achieve business results. They know if the information system is a success.

The recognition of these line people as the principal or primary stakeholders – these are in fact the owners/users – in any information system is a fundamental change in approach or paradigm shift for many organisations. It is however, important to point out that this new approach does not in any way diminish the contribution of the information systems professional to the success of the use of business computing.

However, it does indeed reposition the responsibility for the success of the information system and put it squarely where it should be, with the line managers and users/owners. Information systems professionals remain central stakeholders but their role needs to be refocused rather than changed. They become advisors and educators. Information systems professionals, of course, do not lose their action-orientated role of doers, as they still need to play a central role in making the technology work. But information systems professionals should not be responsible for the innovative processes and practices that are responsible for the benefit creation and delivery. Also the information systems professionals in this way of thinking should not be responsible for justifying the expenditure on the systems. Thus the business case for information systems development needs to be created by the line manager, who will use the system to improve his or her personal or group efficiency and effectiveness.

This new way of understanding the role and function of information systems in organisations does not require information systems departments to be represented on the board of directors. In fact the logic of this new way of thinking is sometimes said to lead to the conclusion that information systems departments should be minimalised. This means that centralised information systems departments should be re-engineered so that information systems resources be placed as close to the line function as possible. This new understanding does not require information systems to be seen as an asset. In fact it may be better to perceive the expenditure on information systems as an operational expense needed to support a particular process or practice.

It will certainly take some time for this new way of understanding the role and function of information systems in organisations to fully register within the business community as a whole. There are many vested interests in keeping the status quo intact and they will take their time to change to a new *modus operandi* such as that described here. However one area in which the impact of this new approach is already being felt is that of presenting business cases for information systems. Business cases are increasingly being prepared on a process-orientated basis, with substantial input from the line managers who will use the technology to improve their work in order to obtain the required benefit streams. This is a major step forward in the use and the management of information systems, which will hopefully lead to far better results being obtained from the employment of the funds required to acquire these systems.

This book presents a framework for the development of a business case. It focuses on how an information system will improve a business process or practice. It goes on to examine how the information system will support the process or practice to produce business benefits. These benefits are quantified by the use of cost-benefit analysis or business case accounting and the business case considers the issues of strategic alignment and risk. Finally the book indicates how a business case can be used as the groundwork for ensuring that the information systems development project will be successfully kept on track.

Dan Remenyi

remenyi@compuserve.com

1 | Why a business case for IT investment?

Our lives teem with numbers, but we sometimes forget that numbers are only tools. They have no soul; they may indeed become fetishes. Many of our most critical decisions are made by computers, contraptions that devour numbers like voracious monsters and insist on being nourished with ever-greater quantities of digits to crunch, digest, and spew back.

P Bernstein, *Against the Gods*, (1996, p.7)

The difficulty lies, not in the new ideas, but in escaping from the old ones.

J. M. Keynes, *The general Theory of Employment, Interest and Money*, (1964)

1.1   Introduction

A new approach to developing a business case for IT investment which will directly help the organisation produce improved results, is long overdue.

Historically, organisations have frequently not bothered to produce a business case or if they have, they have tended to cobble together some financial figures based on a combination of historical records and/or semi-valid assumptions and estimates. Sometimes organisations have produced so-called cost-benefit analysis or even feasibility studies in the form of rather simplistic financial generalisations that have not looked carefully at the business issues involved with or behind the actual IT investment. On the other hand these cost-benefit analysis or feasibility studies have sometimes led to confusion and redundant effort which was clearly demonstrated by Drucker when he said:

We have known for a long time that there is no one right way to analyse a proposed capital investment. To understand it we need at least six analyses: the expected rate of return: the payout period and the investment's expected

*productive life: the discounted present value of all returns through the pro-
ductive lifetime of the investment: the risk in not making the investment or
deferring it: the cost and risk in case of failure: and finally the opportunity
cost.* (Drucker 1988)

Cost-benefit analysis, which may be defined as a financial statement
reflecting the expected expenditure and the possible quantifiable
benefits, does not on its own constitute a complete or comprehensive, or a properly rigorous business case. Cost-benefit analysis is
typically only a relatively small part of a bigger story, and Figure 1.1
shows what might be considered as the relative significance of cost-
benefit analysis in a comprehensively produced business case.

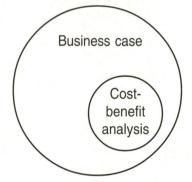

Figure 1.1: Cost-benefit analysis as a sub-set of the business case

The comprehensively produced business case is a greater piece of
work than the relative superficial cost-benefit analysis.

Besides cost-benefit analysis a comprehensively produced business
case needs to consider a number of other issues such as the
stakeholders, the strategic alignment potential of the investment,
the technology involved and the various risks associated with the
project. The reason for this has been well summarised by Laudon
when he said:

*Building an information system, ...an online, distributed, integrated cus-
tomer service system, ...is generally not an exercise in 'rationality'. It is a
statement of war or at the very least a threat to all interests that are in any
way involved with customer service.* (Laudon 1989)

Thus a traditional cost-benefit analysis in a feasibility study is simply not adequate or rigorous enough for an appropriate understanding of the important issues involved in an investment which may go to the heart of the business.[1]

This traditional lack of rigour in business case development has occurred because it has been thought that the key business issues do not easily lend themselves to proper business analysis, let alone sensible financial quantification. This pessimistic view is not as eccentric as it might first sound. It is supported by no less a personage than John Maynard Keynes who is still regarded by many as being one of the greatest economists on the twentieth century. Keynes pointed out as far back as 1936 that the analysis of future business investment was extremely difficult, when he said:

We are merely reminding ourselves that human decision affecting the future, whether personal or political or economic, cannot depend on strict mathematical expectations, since the basis for making such calculations does not exist; and that it is our innate urge to activity which makes the wheels go round, our rational selves choosing between the alternatives as best we are able, calculating where we can, but often falling back for our motive or whim or sentiment or chance. (Keynes 1936)

He went on to say:

Our knowledge of the factors which will govern the yield of an investment some years hence is usually very slight and often negligible. If we speak frankly, we have to admit that our basis of knowledge for estimating the yield ten years hence ... amounts to little and sometimes to nothing; or even five years hence. (Keynes 1936)

There are of course those who would say that the comment of Keynes should have referred to three years hence or even one year hence. This remark goes some way to explain why cost-benefit analysis for IT investments sometimes has so little credability and why it is

---

[1] Of course not all IT investments are of this type. But increasingly organisations want to find IT investment opportunities that will deliver the type of competitive advantage potential referred to here.

sometimes simply seen as satisfying capital budgeting bureaucratic requirements.

Despite Keynes' comments, financial quantification of the costs and benefits related to an investment, even when imperfectly estimated, are useful to managers. But it is important to understand that they are always only part of the greater overall picture.

One of the recurring criticisms of the traditional approach to cost-benefit analysis has been that it was too easy to produce cost-benefit numbers that were based on unsafe assumptions. Thus although a cost-benefit statement may included an impressive array of numbers which purport to represent all the appropriate cost items required to develop an information system, they could be based on totally unfounded guesses or questionable assumptions. This is an even greater problem when it comes to the estimation of the presumed benefits from the IT investment. Because of the fact that some cost-benefit statements have been based on questionable assumptions their credibility has frequently been put in question. Managers, who can sometimes be quite cynical, just do not believe the estimates that are sometimes produced, and this has led to the problem of obtaining the appropriate level of stakeholder commitment. And it is often said that the appropriate level of stakeholder commitment is the single most important factor towards ensuring the success of in IT investment project.

1.2 Business analysis prior to IT investment

Several studies conducted by consultants and academics have found that organisations do not usually perform any formal business analysis prior to IT investment. Research conducted at the end of the 1980s found interesting reasons why organisations did not undertake formal business analysis of IT investments. Managers said that such analysis was not necessary: they said that it was too difficult: they said that it was against their culture and philosophy and just too costly. Clearly such rationalisation is not acceptable in today's fiercely competitive environment. A comprehensive and rigorous business case is being increasingly demanded by senior management prior to IT investment.

1.3   The comprehensive business case

A comprehensive IT investment business case involves a process which looks beyond financial estimates to the central business issues concerning the processes and practices that are the fundamental reasons why organisations invest in IT. This does not imply that financial estimates are not frequently of critical importance, but because of their inability to capture certain issues, financial figures alone are not sufficient for a full business justification of an investment. At the same time it is important to understand that the estimates, financial and other, which are used for investment evaluation are always opinions about the future and are thus not as accurate as is suggested or thought.

Furthermore the traditional approaches to understanding the nature of the costs and the benefits of an IT investment have usually missed an important opportunity, because a well-constructed business case or investment proposal is an important tool in the process of managing the IT investment itself. As IT investments have become increasingly more sophisticated, and as they increasingly require larger and larger amounts of funds, it is important that a comprehensive and professional approach to developing business cases be employed. For example, IT development projects which have enterprise-wide implications are more difficult to manage than single or multiple-function systems and such projects need more planning and management attention. If correctly implemented, an IT business case can provide a foundation or cornerstone from which to measure and manage more successful IT development.

1.4   A business case as a model

An IT business case is a model[2] of what the organisation expects to be able to achieve when it uses IT to support improvements in its process and practices. It is a sophisticated model which is produced to facilitate decision making in the IT management process (Akkermans 1995; Proctor 1995; Corbitt 1995) and to help in this respect with what-if questions (Karlin 1982).

The IT business case model is produced at distinctly different levels. A high-level or macro model is produced which employs general concepts. The purpose of the macro model is to present a conceptual picture which will contextualise the problem or opportunity as well as provide a suggested solution. An intermediate or meso level model will add some detail, and will also express the dimensions of the problem and proposed solution, but will still be expressed primarily in generalities. A detailed or micro level model attempts to be closer to reality and thus to use more specific or life-like representations or values. The primary purpose of the micro model is to understand the detailed impact of the proposed solution or course of action. However, all models are by their nature simplifications of the reality which they represent (Zelm et al 1995). In fact sometimes the simpler the model the more meaningfully it may be used. Complex models may actually cloud the central nature of the issues being studied and thus reduce the explanatory power and consequently the value of the model.

1.5   Definition of a business case

A business case is a justification for pursuing a course of action in an organisational context to meet stated organisational objectives or goals. A business case frequently involves assessing the value of an investment in terms of its potential benefits and the resources

---

[2] A model may be described as a representation of an artefact, a construction, a system or an event or sequence of events. The representation may be abstracted into symbols, equations and numbers, i.e. mathematical expectations; it may consist of a picture or a drawing, or a fabricated likeness such as a model aeroplane, or it may be an expression of a situation or relationship in words.

required to set it up and to sustain it, i.e. its on-going costs. One of the major difficulties in producing a business case is the fact that the benefits of an investment are often a function of the values of the organisation and the executives who are making the investment decisions. Thus a business case will inevitably or inherently have a significant degree of subjectivity associated with it.

1.5.1   Components of a IT business case

A professionally produced business case or investment proposal consists of:

1 a clearly expressed business objective and set of outcomes. These high-level business outcomes need to be comprehensively expressed as a set of opportunities the organisation can take advantage of, or problems that need to be rectified; a list of specific and detailed benefits, their appropriate metrics, measuring methods and responsibility points represented by particular stakeholders, and a justification that the proposed plan will produce an acceptable organisational return. This involves the quantification the contribution made by the outcomes, which requires associating financial numbers or benefit values with outcomes wherever possible;

2 a list of stakeholders and beneficiaries of the investment;

3 a statement of how the proposed IT expenditure will support the corporate strategy;

4 an evaluation of the appropriateness of the technology and operational plan;

5 an evaluation of the risks associated with the investment.

To be of value to an organisation the business case should be expressed in terms of identifiable or quantifiable objectives and actions. Thus it should start with the big picture of what will be achieved by the investment. It should be a multi-dimensional high-level picture of the intentions of the investment. Then a detailed drill-down exercise is needed to establish the precise outcomes,[3]

---

[3] The term 'outcomes' is defined and discussed in Chapter 4. For the moment it is important to note that an IT investment outcome is the way the business will change as a result of the IT-supported intervention.

which can be seen in Figure 1.2 These should be highlighted and expressed in such a way that they can be controlled by appropriate stakeholders, and that it can be ascertained if these outcomes have actually been realised. Chapter 4 shows how this may be done by using a macro, meso and micro model. Thus the business case is a cornerstone of the process of ensuring value-for-money IT investments.

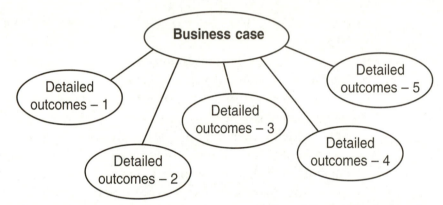

Figure 1.2 The multi-dimensional high-level picture is then drilled-down for detail

In the final analysis a comprehensively produced business case is as much a plan as a justification. It is worth noting that a business case can only be formally produced after a considerable amount of initial work with stakeholders and process analysts has already been done. Thus the business case is not the first step in the process of introducing a new information system.

1.6   Is the IT business case different to other investment?

It is sometimes argued that the IT business case is quite different to business cases for other types of investment. It is believed by some that there is something special about the role of information systems in organisations, which causes their economic justification to be treated differently. It is sometimes said that computers are special; software is intangible; or data or information does not allow itself to be controlled in the same way as other assets. In one sense

1.6 Is the IT business case different to other investment?

this attitude is intrinsically incorrect. Information systems are business tools or instruments in the same way as other business investments and thus they require no less economic justification than any other proposed investment opportunity.

However information systems do exhibit some quite different characteristics to many other business investments which need to be understood and accommodated in an IT business case. These differences include the fact that IT investment opportunities or challenges frequently evolve, not only over long periods of time, but during the relatively short periods[4] while the information system is actually being developed. This means that the final destination of the journey that constitutes the investment is sometimes not known in any detail, at the outset of the work. Specifically, the requirements of an IT development project can end up materially, quite different to what was thought was needed when it first started.

This intrinsic propensity to change is one of the key differences between IT investment projects and other business investment projects.[5] This can be seen as both a major disadvantage, as well as a challenging opportunity.

For many years IT professionals have tried to minimise change during the development process. The derisory term *scope creep* has been coined to describe this propensity to change and considerable energy has been exerted to minimise it, which has sometimes ended in the failure of the project.

---

[4] This question of whether the development period of an information systems development is reactively short may be a contentious one with some readers as IT investments have been known to take several years from the time of specification to the moment they are commissioned.

---

[5] It is not intended to suggest here that other business investment projects do not change during the process of their development. There is much evidence to support the contention that such projects are subject to pressures to change or evolve even while they are being constructed or developed. However it does appear that this tendency or intrinsic propensity to change is especially strong in the IT investment arena.

1.7 Causes of the propensity to require changes IT investments

There are several causes of the propensity to change the requirements of IT investments.

In the first place IT investment projects have traditionally taken fairly long periods of time to complete. Projects lasting two, three or four years have not been uncommon. During this period business conditions and practices change and this, of course, has to be reflected in the IT system being developed. Thus the original specification has to be changed.

But there is an even more demanding challenge involved with IT investments and the system developments they require. The introduction of a new information system requires systems analysis and design work. This is the case whether a small administrative system is being developed, or a large mission-critical system. The process of system analysis and design requires a number of stakeholders to think and re-think their work and how it is performed. This thinking throws up ideas, some that are immediately obvious and useable, but some that take time to mature. The latter can be valuable, but they sometimes are only presented after the project has started. Thus the IT project specification has to be changed.

It is therefore essential that IT investment projects be open to the possibility of continuous change if they are to be successful. This needs to be reflected in the business case.

1.8 The importance of IT business cases today

In today's fiercely competitive environment a comprehensive and rigorous business case is being increasingly demanded by senior management prior to IT investment. There are several reasons why the IT business case has become so important and these relate to the fact that information systems management has come under severe criticism for not producing value for the money invested. This criticism started in the early 1990s and it continues to grow unabated.

The position is well expressed by Keen when he stated that:

Senior executives are caught in a worrisome double bind: ever greater commitments to IT investment are being driven by competitive necessity and discouraged by escalating costs and uncertain benefits. (Keen 1991)

A similar point was made in *Computer Weekly*:

Time has run out for IT managers who act like a protected species. Their three-fold failure to understand the business they are supposed to be part of, to communicate with their business colleagues, and to deliver cost effective systems has led to a collapse of faith in the IT department itself, and a determination by business managers to find alternative solutions to their computing needs. (*Computer Weekly* 1991)

Other critics of IT include Gary Loveman who said in *Computerworld*:

Despite years of technological improvements and investment there is not yet any evidence that information technology is improving productivity or other measures of business performance. (Loveman 1991)

The hard evidence for this was supplied by *Business Week* who claimed that:

Throughout the 80s US businesses invested a staggering $1 trillion in information technology ... Overall, national productivity rose at a puny 1% annual rate. (*Business Week* 1993)

The situation has been made worse for IT managers by a major change of attitude of senior management towards the economics of information systems. This has been well expressed by Lincoln who stated that:

The past few years have seen a marked shift in the attitude of senior executives towards the use of information technology. No longer are expenditures seen as low and investments 'acts of faith'. Now executives require that their information systems are both profitable and can be shown to be profitable. (Lincoln 1986)

Earl has expressed a similar view:

IT is undergoing heavy scrutiny and sometimes radical surgery. IT budgets are being capped or pruned. Headcounts in the IT function are being ra-

tionalised or sold off. IT operations and development are being outsourced. IT directors are being replaced. These are not just reactions to recessionary pressure or changing economics of technology. Chief executives are tiring of IT rhetoric and hype; many of them feel it has been oversold and under delivered. (Earl 1992)

More recently Strassmann pointed out:

It is safe to say that so far nobody has produced evidence to support the popular myth that spending more on information technologies will boost economic performance. (Strassmann 1996)

The enormity of these challenges to information systems management thinking was highlighted by Cane when he reviewed research conducted by Pagoda Associates in London. He pointed out:

Two thirds of big companies are reducing their IT budgets ... and half the companies have cut the number of (IT) staff they employ while some central IT functions have disappeared completely. (Cane 1992)

These reductions in IT budgets and staff represent a new phenomenon, which information systems management needs come to terms with if it is to succeed in the future. In-company IT operations are most certainly under great pressure to be leaner and meaner and in some cases this will require outsourcing and downsizing of some sort.

1.9   Corporate culture is central to a business case

It is critical to note that the approach to be taken in developing a business case is particular to each organisation, and its specific corporate culture.[6] Consequently there is no uniquely correct approach nor is it possible to produce a template which will satisfy all or even most organisations. Despite this there are some helpful checklists discussed in this book. Copies are supplied in the appendices and are available on the World Wide Web at **http://www.bh.com/samples**.

Corporate culture is central and is the determinant of the format of the business case. Possible approaches vary considerably and they

---

[6] In fact some corporate cultures will simply not require the production of a business case.

differ in terms of the input to the business case, how the business case is calculated and processed within the organisation and the sort of results that are obtained.

Some organisations require strong emphasis on detailed financial projections, while others believe that summary financial figures are more than adequate. Some organisations are more interested in descriptions of how their new computer-based business processes will change the way things are done and do not necessarily require these benefits to be quantified in detail.

In some organisations' top management determines the business case and it is handed down for more junior staff to achieve. In other cases the business case is essentially a bottom-up event where the individuals who will actually do the work will create the business case.

However whatever the particular culture the law of parsimony, some-time known as *Occam's razor*,[7] is always an important issue, i.e. a 20-page business case can be substantially more effective than a 200 page treatise. Also the business case should not take weeks or months to develop, nor should it cost a material proportion of the amount to be invested.

1.10 Summary

The current importance that is being attributed to the business case rests on the fact that investment evaluation is seen as a key strategy by which the management of IT investments can be improved.[8] The main issues to which a comprehensively produced business case can contribute include:

1   Facilitating the creation of corporate knowledge and learning in terms of what is really expected from the IT investment and how

---

[7] William of Occam, (c. 1285–1349), a notable English monk and philosopher and theologian coined the expression, which translates into English as "It is vain to do with more what may be done with less". The twentieth century equivalent of this is the KISS principle, which means Keep It Simple, Stupid.

to manage the development project better in order to achieve its objectives; this includes a full assessment of the viability of the IT investment project;

2 An opportunity to acquire the full commitment of the principal stakeholders who will have to play a part in ensuring the success of the IT investment; this includes creating a framework for stakeholder management which is central to ensuring that when the IT investment is commissioned there will be no surprises for any of the major stakeholders;

3 Understanding the risks involved in making the information system deliver the anticipated benefits; this includes putting into place any necessary precautions to reduce the risk or to counter its effects if it actually materialises.

If these three objectives are achieved then the investment in producing the IT business case will have more than paid off. Thus a business case represents a new way of thinking about IT expenditure/investment, which is a major step in the professionalisation of IT project development by providing a foundation or cornerstone from which to measure and manage IT development.

---

[8] The improvements referred to here are not only during the actual IT project development but also during the life cycle of the information system itself. A business case is a valuable management tool from the outset of the IT project right up to the point where it is decommissioned.

2 Preparing an IT business case

The final conclusion is that we know very little, and yet it is astonishing that we know so much, and still more astonishing that so little knowledge can give us so much power.

Bertrand Russell, *The ABC of Relativity* (1925)

We need the courage to let go of the old world, to relinquish most of what we have cherished, to abandon our interpretations about what does and doesn't work.

Margaret Wheatley, *Leadership and the New Science*, (1992).

2.1 Introduction

Before embarking on the process of the preparation of the IT business case it is important to bear in mind that it is more of a corporate cultural process than a strictly technical event. As mentioned in Chapter 1, corporate culture determines of the length and the format of the IT business case, who initiates the business case and how it will be presented and processed in the organisation. Thus the first step is to establish the *house rules* for the IT investment business case. If IT business cases have not been generally in use then it is possible to establish *ab initio* the ground rules for producing them. This type of green-field situation is of course ideal, but in fact most organisations have already been using some sort of approach to producing a business case, or at least a feasibility study, or cost-benefit analysis, and it will probably be necessary to some extent to follow the precedents set up by the rules underpinning these approaches. Furthermore corporate culture will determine what issues are important to the organisation and which issues are not. Although, it is sometimes thought that facts and figures are unassailable, in most cases they are not. This has been pointed out by

Stephen Gould, who although writing in a more general vein made a point that is relevant to business when he said:

Facts are not pure and unsullied bits of information; culture also influences what we see and how we see it. (Gould 1992)

It also needs to be remembered that before an IT business case can be developed a considerable amount of background work will already need to have been done. This background work will have involved some degree of validation of the proposed new system. It may have included some process modelling and it will certainly have involved in-depth discussions with the principal stakeholders. Depending on the proposed IT investment this background research work may take several weeks or even months before it is possible to proceed with the development of the IT business case itself.

Although there are several different approaches to IT business case development any comprehensive IT business case needs to address five major areas or elements of concern.

2.2 The elements of an IT business case

The five elements to a comprehensively produced IT investment business case are the business outcome, stakeholder management, strategic alignment, technology issues and project and system risks. These five elements are shown in Figure 2.1 below. Each of these elements is part of the process of preparing an IT investment business case and that process will be described in Figure 2.4.

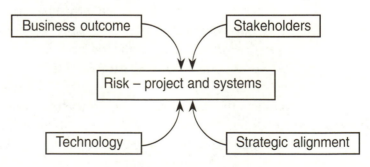

Figure 2.1 An overview of the IT Business case

Each of these five elements require detailed analysis which forms a substantial section of the IT business case. Chapters 4, 5 6, 7, 8 and 9 describe how these elements of the IT business case need to be produced. Chapter 4 discusses the business outcome, and the material in this chapter is supported by a detailed discussion of business case accounting in Chapter 9. Chapter 5 discusses the question of stakeholders. Chapter 6 discusses the issues related to strategic alignment, while Chapter 7 discusses the subject of the technology. Chapter 8 looks at the important question of the risk associated with an IT project.

Thus there are five distinct parts or modules to the IT investment business case. Each module needs to be developed separately by the appropriate stakeholders. As described in Chapter 5 there are three groups of primary stakeholders. These are the users/owners, the IT professionals and the finance and administration staff.

All five modules of the IT investment business case need to be completed with input from all three of these groups of stakeholders on a collaborative basis. However, the users/owners need to assume overall responsibility for the production and the final integration of the IT business case.

The business outcome module should be produced primarily by the users/owners with some significant help from the finance and administration staff with the business case accounting section. The strategic alignment module needs to be prepared by a group comprising the users/owners as well as members of the top management team and the strategic planning group. The stakeholder module should be produced primarily by the original proposer or sponsor of the IT investment. This individual or group of individuals needs to be either part of the users/owners, or be closely aligned with them. The technology module needs to be prepared by the IT professionals in collaboration with the users/owners and the risk management module will require input from all the different primary stakeholders. The four arrows in Figure 2.1, flowing from the four corner boxes into the risk box have been drawn to reflect the fact that their composition directly affects the risk profile of the IT investment. Any changes in any of these four issues will most probably directly affect the risk profile.

In this chapter some of the background issues that are of importance to all of these elements, and without which the IT investment business case cannot be developed, are discussed. These background issues include consensus, acceptance of change, the importance of phased delivery, etc.

2.3   The consensus issue

An important aspect of the IT business case is that it is a vehicle for producing a consensus between the principal stakeholders as to how the IT project will proceed. This consensus of understanding and commitment will have been arrived at through a process of research, evaluations, discussions and dialogues whereby differences and conflicts will have been resolved. This may have required several reiterations of the IT investment business case document before agreement has been reached.

In producing the business case, the philosophical underpinnings or the values of the organisation and the principal stakeholders need to be articulated, understood and agreed. Consensus is central to the successful implementation of an IT investment as disagreements can lead to major difficulties with the project and in fact cause it to fail. In fact an IT project should not be commenced until there is a high degree of consensus between all the principal stakeholders. When consensus is not obtained then the risk profile the project faces is substantially heightened.

2.3.1   Differences in values

Some organisations have a high regard for the value delivered by their IT and the role it can play in the success of their business. Others take a different view, which was well demonstrated by Lacity and Hirschheim, when they pointed out:

only two of the thirteen companies that participated in the study agree that their IS departments are critical to corporate success. The remaining eleven companies all see their IS departments as necessary, but burdensome, cost pits. (Lacity and Hirschheim 1995)

Value, and especially IT value is indeed a difficult question. This has has been expressed succinctly by Keen when he said:

Many a scholar, consultant and practitioner has tried to devise a reliable approach to measuring the business value of IT at the level of the firm, none has succeeded. (Keen 1991, p162)

There is no simple answer to this difficult question and this is one of the reasons why a comprehensive IT investment business case is necessary.

Another way in which corporate values can differ in respect to IT relates to the issue of change or creeping commitment. Although most organisations do not like change, especially in respect of its IT developments, it is crucial to understand that change is actually unavoidable. Denial of this fact is frequently lethal to IT projects. Another way of looking at this issue is to say that IT project success is a moving target. Clearly system requirements evolve over time and the organisation of an IT project needs to accommodate this.

2.3.2 The acceptance of change

The lack of acceptance of the inevitability of change by information systems developers is at the core of IT investment failure. Projects set up in such a way that they do not accommodate any changes to the specification of requirements during the development phase of the project frequently get out of step with what is really required and when it is attempted to deliver or commission these systems they are unacceptable to the user/owner. Accommodating such changes to requirements has plagued the IT profession for years and it is generally considered that it is not a simple matter to ensure that systems specifications remain relevant, especially when the development period is long i.e. extends over a year or more. Thus the acceptance of change by information systems developers is at the heart of sound IT project delivery.

At the core of the idea of the acceptance of change is the notion of the information systems outcome, which may be defined as the business result, including the benefit stream of the information system after it has been successfully commissioned and implemented. Using a comprehensive approach to an IT business case, the information system is defined in broad business terms, largely in terms of benefits, which in some cases might be quite general in nature. The term *outcome space* is used to describe these business benefits.

The IT business case may be understood as part of the process by which an information systems development project proceeds from the initiation point to an acceptable location in the outcome space[1] in order to achieve suitable benefits for the organisation.

As the IT project development proceeds, a series of checks are made, which are referred to in business literature as formative evaluations.[2] These checks are used to ensure that the project remains within the boundaries that will eventually lead the information system to a point in the outcome space and thus deliver the required benefit stream. This is shown in Figure 2.2. The project initialisation requires a high-level definition and description of the major characteristics of the outcome space. The outcome space is a general description of the way in which the originators of the IT investment, probably the primary stakeholder, believes the business processes and practices which will change, as a result of the IT investment, will deliver better business performance.

It is important not to burden the high-level definitions and descriptions of the outcome space with too much specific detail and it is essential to be prepared to allow systems specification changes to be

---

[1] The term 'outcome space' refers to a set of possible outcomes of a IT investment all of which would be regarded as satisfactory. The outcome space is defined in terms of the way in which the business may change as a result of the way the IT investment is used to support new or refined business processes and practices.

---

[2] The concept of formative evaluation is explained in detail in Chapter 3. However, in brief, formative evaluation is a process by which a policy is established that will help lead to the achievement of the project's objectives.

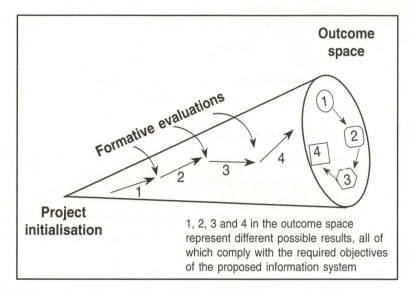

Figure 2.2: Outcome space and formative evaluation

identified and accommodated while the system developments are in progress. This of course means that all the details of the IT investment business case cannot be regarded as being set in concrete but rather as a possible scenario to which the organisation and the principal stakeholders wish to aim.

This preparedness to recognise the inevitability of change may be regarded as a post-modern[3] idea underpinning the use of the IT business case in this way. Employing values and concepts such as contingency, continuous participative evaluation, co-evolution is perfectly valid for activities within the information systems environment.

---

[3] The author has taken some licence in the use the term *post-modernism*. According to the *Fontana Dictionary of Modern Thought*, 'post-modernism is an increasingly familiar if still controversial term for defining or suggesting the overall character or direction of experimental tendencies in Western arts, architecture, etc. since the 1940s or 1950s and particularly more recent developments associated with post-industrial society.' In the context of this book post-modernism is used to suggest new and somewhat experimental directions in management thinking, especially as it applies to information systems development. These rely on, *inter alia*, the contingency notion, which recognises that organisations cannot stop the world from changing during the period of information systems development. The best such organisations can do is adapt quickly.

Although the post-modernist concept as it is applied to information systems development concentrates on a number of issues, one of the most important is the contingent mind-set to systems development. In simple terms this means that information systems goalposts[4] may change and developers need to be prepared for this.

2.3.3 The importance of phased delivery

Tied in with the notion of the outcome space and formative evaluation is the fact that phased delivery of an information system is essential. By phased delivery is meant that the project outcomes are divided up into a series of outputs and that these outputs are delivered over a period of time and not held back for a one final big event or big-bang delivery.

Big- bang delivery is increasingly believed to be problematic for project success. Thus it is necessary to divide the project up into manageable parts and implement a continuous programme of delivery, whereby the stakeholders' commitment to the project as each part is delivered is ensured. If at any time the stakeholder commitment diminishes then the validity of the project is thrown into question. Formative or participatory or learning evaluation is helpful as a means of ensuring this commitment.

2.3.4 Stakeholder management of IT

The idea of the management of IT projects by its primary stakeholders relates to the fact that information systems per se do not produce benefits. Information systems are capital investments,

---

[4] Generally goalpost changes are usually regarded as aberrations, which where possible, need to be avoided, and significant management trauma is experienced as the new goals are missed, and targets are not achieved. There is now a growing recognition that the assumptions behind the static nature of goals are not only unrealistic, but are detrimental to organisational progress and to the achievement of significant benefits which most initiatives or investments should produce. These old unrealistic assumptions of stasis which have largely incorrectly defined management reality and thus influenced behaviours, need to change if we are to remain in touch with the rapid pace of business, social and political change faced by organisations as they enter the twenty-first century.

which if used appropriately by line staff and business executives can assist people make changes to processes and practices, which will in turn make these individuals more efficient and effective. It is the improvement in the efficiency and effectiveness of these individuals that causes the organisation to experience a benefit stream. In turn the new benefit stream will be reflected in the organisation's profit and return on investment calculations.

Without an understanding of the nature of information systems the hunt for benefits can be a frustrating business. Figure 2.3 shows the chain of events from the changes to processes and practices to the improved profit and increased return on investment (ROI).

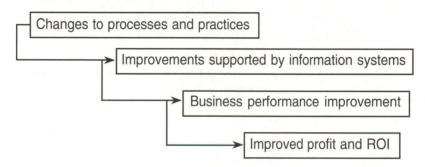

Figure 2.3: How profit and ROI are improved by IT

Only if the principal stakeholders i.e. those who will be using the new IT are fully committed, and only if they are actually managing the project, is there any real likelihood of success. Of course even with stakeholder management, project success is never guaranteed.

2.3.5 Accuracy of estimation

In the IT business case there will invariably be a series of financial projections estimating costs and benefits. The estimation of these costs, the benefits and the other variables can be relatively straightforward. These estimations can be based on quotations or on historical experience or on expert judgement.

Accuracy in project estimates is always welcome, but accurate financial estimates are not the main issue. Sometimes estimates that are within parameters such as plus or minus 10% can be perfectly adequate. A higher degree of accuracy may be too expensive and take too much time and sometimes concentration on accuracy is a distraction and is not really essential in the production of adequate cost and benefit estimates for an IT investment project.

2.3.6   Strategic alignment

The organisation's corporate strategy is of central importance to its effective use of IT investments. Strategic mismatches or misalignments are major causes of IT project failure and any professionally produced IT business case needs to rigorously address this subject. It is not an easy matter to ensure that IT investment is aligned with corporate strategy for a number of reasons including the fact that corporate strategy may not be known to the proposers or sponsors or users/owners of the system. Furthermore it is possible that the corporate strategy may change during the period when the IT investment project is under development.

Strategic alignment is fully discussed in Chapter 6.

2.3.7   Technology

No matter how sound or how good the proposed IT intervention is from a business perspective it is necessary to take a careful look at the technology issues to see if the project is really viable. To do this it is necessary to develop a technology feasibility statement that outlines the various technology platforms and components required i.e. hardware, software, communications, etc. The technology feasibility statement needs to be completed by information technology specialists either from the organisation, by consultants or from outsourcers.

The issue of technology is fully discussed in Chapter 7.

2.3.8   Risk – project and system

IT risk can be defined as the propensity of the actual costs and outputs of the IT development to vary from the original business case. In simple terms this can be regarded as being equivalent to *what can go wrong*. It is of prime importance for a business case to address the risk issue, as without doing this the business case is at best incomplete and at worst a misunderstanding of what may be expected during the project.

The issue of risk is discussed in Chapter 8.

2.4   An IT investment business case as a process

Although the results of IT investment business case is presented as a document, its production or development is best understood as a business process in its own right. The activities required in this business process are shown in Figure 2.4.

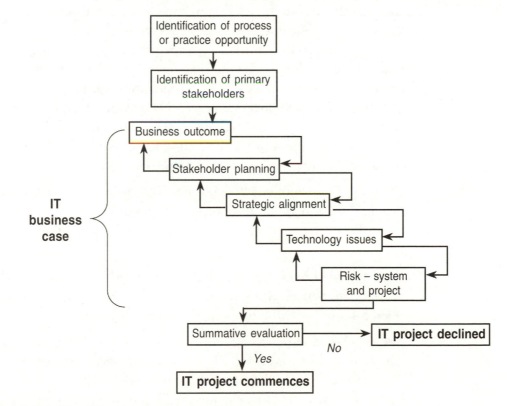

Figure 2.4: The IT business case as a process

This process has three major activity groups which are:

1 The identification of the business process or practice opportunity;

2 The identification of the stakeholders who will work on the development of the business case;

3 The production of the business case itself which requires reiteration.

This process requires input from various stakeholders mentioned above. The different stakeholders may have quite different views as to how they see the proposed new or enhanced IT supported business process or practice. Sometimes these different stakeholders may even have conflicting objectives. Where there are differences and conflicts the probability of IT investment success is low. It is part the IT investment business case process to attempt to resolve any such differences and conflicts. The required approach here is to hold a series of discussions during which all the different views are aired. Through the process of skilled negotiations, gaps may be closed and different stakeholders' requirements may be brought closer together. The series of feedback loops shown in Figure 2.4 suggests that the development of the different parts of the body of the business case may requires several reiterations.

Once the IT investment business case has been developed a decision has to be made whether or not to proceed with the IT investment. This is done by summative evaluation which is discussed in Chapter 3.

If the IT investment business case is considered sound then the IT project commences, if the IT investment business case is not considered sound then the proposed IT project is declined.

The process required to develop the IT investment business case may take weeks or even months to conclude and may cost the organisation a non-trivial amount of money. Thus there needs to be a budget for the costs of producing the IT investment business case.

2.5   Summary

A comprehensively produced business case for an IT investment serves two distinct purposes. In the first place it is the basis for making a decision as to whether or not to invest in the proposed project. For this reason it is necessary to consider in detail the five dimensions or issues shown in Figure 2.1 i.e. business outcomes, stakeholders, strategic alignment, technology issues and project and system risks. It is important that these issues are considered in a holistic manner and this is well demonstrated by the jigsaw diagram used in Figure 2.5.

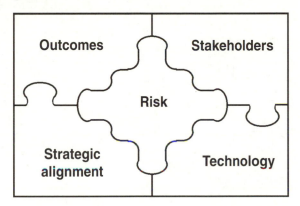

Figure 2.5: The integration of the five issues central to the business case

In the second place the business case should be central to the process of managing an IT project, with the business case being used to obtain stakeholder commitment. Stakeholders' commitment and their involvement in the project management are of fundamental importance to any IT project. Perhaps the single most important reason why IT projects fail is the lack of stakeholder commitment.

Thus a business case should not simply be a document which is produced to approve or authorise an IT project, but rather it should be at the centre of the IT project management.

3 | The art of evaluation

The word 'belief' is a difficult thing for me. I don't believe. I must have a reason for a certain hypothesis. Either I know a thing, and then I know it— I don't need to believe it.

Carl Jung, *interview,* (1959)

'One can't believe impossible things', said Alice. 'I dare say you haven't had much practice,' said the Queen. 'When I was your age, I always did it for half-an-hour a day. Why, sometimes I've believed as many as six impossible things before breakfast.'

Lewis Carroll, *Through the Looking Glass,* (1872)

3.1 Introduction

The IT business case can be regarded as part of the general IT evaluation activity within the organisation and one which is increasingly seen as central to the delivery of quality IT management. It is not easy to ensure that any activity is being performed well if there are not mechanisms in place to monitor how that activity is living up to the exceptions of its consumers. This is the role of IT evaluation activities and the IT investment business case sets the standard to which the IT evaluation activities need to be compared.

Furthermore to understand the mechanisms behind the IT business case it is necessary to examine the concepts and techniques used in evaluation. These become especially important when the IT investment business case is used as part of the IT project management process.

Most of the concepts and techniques used in evaluation are not new. Many of them have been used in the public sector for many years. However they are increasingly being used in business and management and recently they have begun to play an important role in IT management.

3.2 Evaluation and the business case

At the heart of an IT business case is an evaluation of the investment. This evaluation needs to address business issues, financial issues, strategic issues, stakeholder issues, technical issues and risk issues. In addressing this range of different issues it is essential to have a clear definition and understanding of what is involved in evaluation.

Evaluation is a process that is intuitively known, or at least instinctively undertaken by just about everyone. It is either a conscious or instinctive reviewing process, which assesses the value[1] of an object or the merit of a particular situation. Thus cricket teams, motor cars, schools and universities and hospitals, summer holidays as well as business investments are evaluated at sometime, in some way. More formally evaluation according to Scriven is:

usually defined as the determination of the worth or value of something ... judged according to appropriate criteria, with those criteria explicated and justified. (Scriven 1991)

Evaluation and the techniques associated with it may be used in many different aspects of business and management. In fact, Shadish *et al* in the opening chapter of their book state:

We can evaluate anything – including evaluation itself. (Shadish *et al.* 1991)

During the past few decades, evaluation has been increasingly associated with management in an attempt to improve economic productivity from both an efficiency and effectiveness point of view

---

[1] The Oxford Dictionary gives the following definition for evaluation: 'the action of working out the value of something'. Evaluation is a weighing up process to assess the value of an object or the merit of a situation and it is on this basis that the definition used in this book was developed. Evaluation is a process incorporating understanding, assessment and sometimes measurement of some sort against a set of criteria (Symons 1991). It is most important to note that this does not necessarily mean financial measurement. It can also relate to the determination of the worth of an object. In the context of this book the evaluation process directly supports and enhances the management decision making process.

(Picciotto 1999). In the business environment evaluation is at the heart of all activity. In fact according to Love:

...... evaluation began to be recognised as an indispensable tool for managers and an essential part of the management process. (Love 1991)

While the concept of corporate or business evaluation has been in existence for some years, the evaluation of information systems has not traditionally been a major issue. The relentless evolution of computers in business more and more towards mission-critical applications and the changing attitudes of management to the large amounts of money spent on IT have resulted in a large amount of managerial concern about value for money issues. With this there has been a change in approach towards information systems evaluation and senior management has increasingly demanded detailed ex-ante and ex-post evaluation (see section 3.3.2).

There is now a greater awareness that information systems can radically transform the way in which organisations do business, both in terms of established business practices and the work environment for the organisation's staff (Chelimsky 1997). It is generally recognised that information systems change the social structure of the organisation. According to Farbey *et al.*:

At the heart of IT's new role is the wider range of benefits IT can now bring. Traditionally IT applications reduce costs but this does not transform business processes, inter-organisational networks and business scope. (Farbey *et al.* 1993)

However the evaluation of the impact of a new information system often poses a significant problem. Information systems are not seen as simply a tool to record transactions and process data, but as a competitive weapon which can change an industry structure, alter key competitive forces, and affect an organisation's choice of strategy. These types of investments require large sums of money and there is growing concern among both IS and business professionals as to whether the benefits of computing are being realised, and thus the need for increased investment in IS evaluation.

Despite the increased role of IT in organisations and increased expenditure there is considerable doubt as to whether sizeable IT investments are proving to be justifiable. Establishing or measuring the business value of computer systems have perplexed managers and researchers for several years (Hitt and Brynjolfsson 1994). A number of studies present contradictory evidence as to whether the expected benefits of computers have materialised. And thus with increasing investment in information technology, together with claims of gaining competitive advantage, there is still some doubt as to how IT is giving strategic advantage and whether the benefits of information systems are being realised (Lincoln 1986; Benjamin *et al* 1990; Remenyi *et al* 1995). As a result of this, many practitioners feel that IS evaluation and IT business case development have become a key management issue.

The production of a business case is the first step in applying this evaluation thinking to information systems management in the organisation. In this context evaluation is a process incorporating understanding, assessment and sometimes measurement (Mayne and Zapio-Goni 1997). It is either a conscious or tacit process that aims to establish the value or the contribution made by a particular situation. It can also relate to the determination of the worth of an object.

Allied to this is the concept of the purpose of the evaluation exercise. This is articulated by Walsham who states that:

A key element of the evaluation ...is the purpose for which the evaluation is being carried out; this purpose may be explicitly stated or may be implicit. (Walsham 1993)

From a business point of view the purpose of the IT business case evaluation should be clear. The evaluation process directly supports management decision-making and its primary objective is the maximisation of benefits potentially available due to a project's investment, and in so doing adds value to the organisation as a whole.

But of course there is always another side to business processes and the purpose of an evaluation, especially an information systems evaluation, may not always be obvious. According to Farbey et al.:

The process of appraising new investment is always a political process in so far as it touches on the diverse interests of many people and groups. (Farbey et al 1993)

Thus the context in which the IT business case evaluation is conducted needs to be fully understood.

The evaluation of information systems is a relatively complex matter, requiring a considerable amount of understanding of the organisation and the main players and actors involved. According to Hopwood the evaluation process may be regarded as a management information system in its own right. He states:

Be aware that the evaluation exercise is itself a complex information processing activity, subject to all the problems and opportunities which characterise this area. (Hopwood 1983)

3.3 Dimensions of evaluation

Evaluation may be performed in many different ways and may be said to have several different dimensions and application types. In very broad terms it may be said that evaluation may be subjective or objective. Evaluation may be qualitative or quantitative or in fact it may include aspects of both qualitative and quantitative techniques. The comprehensive approach to the development of an IT investment business case as described in this book may be regard as a hybrid approach employing aspects of both qualitative or quantitative techniques.

3.3.1 Types of evaluation

There are several different types of evaluation: ex-ante and ex-post evaluation; formative and summative evaluation; quantitative and qualitative evaluation approaches; subjective and objective techniques. Each of these is appropriate in different circumstances. There are a number of taxonomies that allow the categorisation of evaluation techniques and methodologies. The following sections examine two of the primary categories of evaluation, which are ex-ante and ex-post evaluations and summative and formative evaluations.

An IT business case is by its nature an ex-ante evaluation. However it will be argued later in this book that an IT business case should not be simply evaluated once. Thus by using an IT business case as part of the project management process some aspects of ex-post evaluation may be required.

3.3.2 Ex-ante and ex-post evaluation

Predictive evaluations performed to forecast and evaluate the impact of future situations are sometimes referred to as ex-ante evaluations. Post-implementation evaluations that assess the value of existing situations are sometimes referred to as ex-post evaluations. Ex-ante evaluations are normally performed using financial estimates that may be either single point estimates of costs and benefits or range estimates of such figures. In either case this type of analysis attempts to forecast the outcome of the information systems investment in terms of an indicator or set of indicators such as the payback, the net present value (NPV) or the internal rate of return (IRR), to mention only three.

The purpose of ex-ante evaluation is to support systems justification. Systems justification, which is sometimes confused with evaluation, implies first an evaluation and then the activity of justification, showing that the information system is appropriate for the particular business context. The purpose of ex-post evaluation is to assess and confirm, or refute, the value of a realised design or a completed action. The ex-post or the post-implementation evaluations investigate and analyse the current system to examine 'what is' against some previously suggested situation. This is done to confirm the value of the system and support operational decisions about improvements. Ex-post evaluations can be made on the basis of financial indicators such as those described for the ex-ante situation above or they can be made using other non-financial measures such as user satisfaction surveys.

Ex-ante or predictive evaluations on which IT business cases are dependent are complex. The evaluator has to understand the existing system in order to predict and understand the future system, as well as be able to estimate the potential impact of the future situation. On the other hand ex-ante evaluations only require estimates of likely costs and benefits while ex-post evaluation require actual costs and actual benefits which are sometimes very difficult to determine.

3.3.3   Formative and summative evaluation

Evaluation activities may also be categorised as formative and summative. Formative evaluation, which is sometimes referred to as learning evaluation (Senge 1992), has been explained by Finne *et al.* as:

... Formative evaluation approaches typically aim at improving program performance, take place while the program is in operation, rely to a large extent on qualitative data and are responsive to the focusing needs of program owners and operators. (Finne *et al.*1995)

This theme is expanded by Patton, who points out:

Formative evaluations are conducted for the purpose of improving programs in contrast to those evaluations which are done for the purpose of making basic decisions about whether or not the program is effective. (Patton 1980)

Thus formative evaluation is central to sound information systems management processes and practice. If used correctly formative evaluation will lead to a much higher rate of information systems project success.

The term formative is taken from the word form, 'to mould by discipline and education'. Formative evaluation is viewed as an iterative evaluation and decision-making process continually influencing the social programme and influencing the participants, with the overall objective of achieving a more acceptable and beneficial outcome from the programme. Summative evaluation on the other hand, derived from the word sum, is viewed as an act of evaluation assessing the final (sum) impact of the programme. IT business cases are by their nature initially summative. Adelman (1996) points out that summative and formative are conditions of the evaluator in contrast to process and product, which are conditions of the evaluation.

It is recognised that in systems development both formative and summative evaluation takes place. Hewett describes this:

As applied to the development of computer systems, formative evaluation involves monitoring the process and products of system development and gathering user feedback for use in the refinement and further system development. Summative evaluation involves assessing the impact, usability and effectiveness of the system; the overall performance of user and system. (Hewett 1986)

He goes on to point out that in systems development these two types of evaluation are required in mixes of different proportions at different stages in the development cycle. In practice there is an overlap of the two conditions. The adoption of either summative or formative evaluation approaches depends on the preferences and needs of those performing the evaluation of the information system as well as the phase of the IT project which is being evaluated. The use of an IT business case in order to improve project success requires a formative evaluation approach.

3.3.3.1 IT investemnt business case and summative evaluation

When the IT investment business case document has been prepared, a judgement has to be made as to whether or not to proceed with the IT project or decline the suggested opportunity. This judgement requires a summative evaluation which leads to a *yes* or a *no* answer.

3.3.3.2 IT investment business case and formative evaluation

Once the IT investement business case has been accepted and the IT project has begun, formative evaluation has a major role to play in ensuring that the IT project remains on track and delivers a satisfactory result.

3.3.4 Formative evaluation and participation

Formative evaluation is not only about measuring the contribution, but also about the inclusion of the views and opinions of a wide range of the stakeholders. This type of evaluation does not stop at summary statistics, but probes the reality behind the numbers in order to understand what is really going on, i.e. what is being achieved, what is to be achieved and what the current and potential problems are. Adelman suggests:

that formative admits more representational equity than summative and giving equal voice to all stakeholders also admits diversity. (Adelman 1996)

Thus formative evaluation is sometime referred to as participatory evaluation. Also the same process is sometimes called learning evaluation as is explained by Brunner and Guzman when they said:

Participatory evaluation is an educational process through which the social groups produce action-oriented knowledge about their reality, clarify and articulate their norms and values, and reach a consensus about future action. (Brunner and Guzman 1989)

The terms formative and summative do not in themselves imply participation for formative evaluation and non-participation for summative evaluation. From its definition 'moulding by discipline and education' there is at least an expectation that stakeholders are involved in a formative evaluation process. But it is also clear that a participatory summative evaluation can take place.

3.3.5 Formative evaluation and reiteration

Formative evaluation is a reiterative process whereby a system's requirements are refined or co-evolved in a controlled manner. Formative evaluation will take place many times during the tenure of an IT project. The actual number of times will depend upon the type of project and the environment in which it is being pursued. At the end of each formative evaluation the business case may be changed to reflect new circumstances and the project will, hopefully, continue with a new or adjusted set of objectives and requirements. Figure 3.1 shows the reiterative nature of this activity.

At the heart of a business case is an evaluation of the investment. This evaluation needs to address business issues, financial issues and technical issues. In addressing this range of different issues it is essential to have a clear definition and understanding of what is involved in evaluation.

3.4 Other evaluation issues

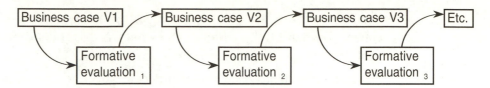

Figure 3.1: Reiterative process of formative evaluation

3.4 Other evaluation issues

There are several other evaluation issues that need to be understood as part of an IT business case. These issues include the question of whether the evaluation should be performed on quantitative or qualitative evidence and whether the evaluation should be continuous or periodic.

In general the use of both quantitative and qualitative evidence is preferable. The financial estimates that are part of the micro model in the outcome section of the IT business case will be intrinsically quantitative where investment statistics such as payback, return on investment and net present values, etc., are calculated. This is discussed in detail in Chapter 9. There may also be other survey type evidence such as the responses to questionnaires, which will also be somewhat quantitative. But in addition to these numbers there will also be opinions concerning the strategic alignment, the stakeholder management, etc., which will be qualitative. These opinions are just as important as the quantitative part of the IT business case.

Although the IT business case is generally only produced at the outset of the project[2] it can be reviewed a number of times. In fact it may be argued that the IT business case should be reviewed at each major milestone during the project. This would be a periodic approach to the review of the IT business case. There is also the argument

---

[2] The notion that the IT business case is generally only produced at the outset of the project is in some respects rather idealistic. Sometimes projects are started without any business case and after a period of time management calls for a business case to justify the continued IT development. Some consultants report that they have been working on a project for several years before a business case was required.

that the IT business case should be under continuous review in the sense that any stakeholder could ask for a review session whenever they feel it is appropriate to so do. This would be referred to a continuous approach to the IT business case evaluation.

3.5 A professional approach to the evaluation process

Professional evaluation is not a simple matter that can be conducted quickly and simply. Evaluation, especially as it is practised in the preparation and use of a business case for an IT investment, is a management process requiring a high degree of knowledge and discipline. The evaluation should focus on a full range of business outcomes which include direct business benefits as well as their financial estimates. It is important to include both tangible and intangible benefits. Tests of materiality and credibility need to be applied especially to intangible benefits and these are discussed in Chapter 9.

In additon the evaluation needs to be conducted by all the primary or major stakeholders. Without involving the opinions of all the major stakeholders the business case will simply not be useful.

3.6 Summary

Evaluation theory has its roots in social or public sector programme assessment, which was initiated more than one hundred years ago, and has today become an important field of study in its own right, with distinct implications for business and management performance. Evaluation theory is central to the production of a comprehensive business case for IT investment in that evaluation techniques underpin all aspects of the production of the IT business case.

The IT investment business case will be an ex-ante, summative evaluation which will require a significant degree of participation from all the important stakeholders. The IT investment business case may well have to go through several reiterations before the process of producing this document is complete.

Although the production of a business case for an IT investment can be expensive and time consuming, there is frequently a large payback associated with this activity[3]. Of the several different levels of payback to be derived from a business case, the facilitation of corporate learning is regarded by many to be the most positive and perhaps the most important reason for undertaking this evaluation work. Thus a business case for an IT investment not only helps decide whether to proceed with a particular IT opportunity and assist the capital rationing process in order to prioritise projects, but also creates a platform from which the organisation can learn to manage IT projects more successfully.

---

[3] It is not possible to say how long it should take to develop a comprehensive IT investment business case as this will clearly depend on the precise nature of the IT investment. However except for very small and simple IT investments it is likely that a well produced business will require several person weeks of effort. On the question of the cost of a comprehensive IT investment business case, many practitioners have made the point that it is worthwhile spending a material amount of money on this activity if it can ensure a more sound approach to the IT project when it is finally approved.

4 | The business outcome

Nowadays people know the price of everything and the value of nothing.
Oscar Wilde, *The Picture of Dorian Gray*, (1891)

We inhabit a world that is always subjective and shaped by our interactions with it. Our world is impossible to pin down, constantly and infinitely, more interesting than we ever imagined.
Margaret Wheatley, *Leadership and the New Science*, (1992)

4.1 Introduction

Traditional feasibility studies or information system justifications tended to be one-dimensional statements focusing on financial estimates. This approach was always seen as a limitation but it was often felt that it was too difficult, would take too long and be too complicated to present a more rounded evaluation of the information systems investment proposal. Today at the heart of the comprehensive IT business case is the understanding that financial numbers alone are not good enough for making information systems investment decisions and that a more holistic approach is much more appropriate.

Thus when using the comprehensive approach to producing an IT business case it is necessary to consider multiple views – a view of the investment outcomes (including financial cost and benefits estimates), a view of the degree of strategic alignment inherent in the investment, a view of the stakeholders, a view of the technology to be employed and a view of the project and system risks involved. Looking again at the overview of the IT business case (Figure 4.1) it can be seen that the risks are at the centre of the project.

These five views are the most important perspectives that need to be taken into account when an information systems investment proposal is presented. Notice that the five views of the IT investment are interconnected through the project risk which is the central issue.

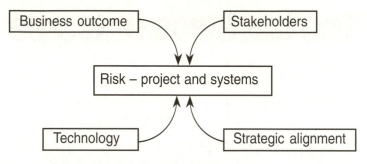

Figure 4.1 An overview of the IT Business case

These views or perspectives need to be reduced to documents that are not trivial to complete, but neither are they so complicated as to be burdensome. Each view needs to be developed separately by the appropriate stakeholder in association with, or in consultation with the other primary stakeholders. This collaboration is important as each of these sets of issues have a bearing on each other.

4.2 Outcome statement or statements

Before discussing the development of a outcome statement it is important to be clear on the definition of both an outcome and an output of an IT investment. The outcome of an IT investment may be defined as the desired effect of an intervention or change to a business process or practice. It is a business result, which has a measurable impact on the performance of the organisation. The output of an IT investment is the physical change to a business process or practice which will lead to the business result as required in the outcome.

IT investment outcomes need to be expressed as statements. The outcome statement is a comprehensive statement or sometimes a set of statements of the expected results in precise business terms of the IT initiative. It relates to the primary business problem or opportunity and represents in quite specific terms the vision of how the business will perform when the IT opportunity is realised. It is derived or developed directly from the primary business problem or opportunity statement. So, for example, if the information system is targeted at changing the profile of the company's customer base from having many small customers to a more restricted group of large highly creditworthy customers then the outcome can be expressed as: *more sales revenues on fewer invoices from well-established customers of good financial standing who pay promptly.*

Any IT investment opportunity may have several outcomes. Thus another expected outcome, in the above example, could be that the business relationship with the customer will be closer or tighter and that the salesperson will call more frequently on the customer and spend more time with them, which will result on more sales per invoice.

As the business outcome is at the heart of the IT investment business case, a comprehensive statement or set of statements of business outcome will need to be thoroughly developed and will thus consist of three distinct levels or components.[1] These components, which are shown in Figure 4.2, are referred to as the macro model, the meso model and the micro model.

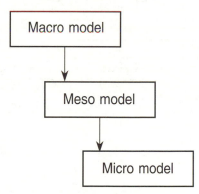

Figure 4.2: The three steps in the business outcome

These three models need to be produced sequentially beginning with the macro model, then proceeding to the meso model and

---

[1] It is possible that the business outcome dimension could require as much as 20 to 40 per cent of the effort of the entire IT business case exercise.

finally completing the micro model.[2] The detail required in each of these models grows from perhaps as little as a few paragraphs for the macro model to maybe a dozen pages or so for the micro model.

It is important that the macro model is fully concluded and agreed to by the stakeholders before the meso model and the micro model are produced. Misunderstandings with regard to the macro model are one of the more common causes of project failure.

4.2.1 The macro model

A macro model is a high level statement in words and diagrams of the proposed organisational intervention or change. A macro model should contain a statement of the problem or opportunity, what will be done by who, when to take advantage of it, and what the expected outcome or business result will be. A macro model will typically require the seven items of information listed in Figure 4.3.

	Macro model	Details
1.1	Name of the proposed intervention	*Limit this to around 10 words*
1.2	State the perceived problem or opportunity	*Limit this to around 100 words*
1.3	Why is it a problem or opportunity?	*Limit this to around 75 words*
1.4	What is the nature of the intervention?	*Limit this to around 50 words*
1.5	What will be the result of the intervention?	*Limit this to around 75 words*
1.6	Identify the users/owner	*List up to five possible users/owners of the intervention*
1.7	State the timeframe required	

Figure 4.3: The macro model form to be completed

---

[2] Although the business outcome modelling is generally regarded as the place to start the IT investment business case, the three models cannot be finalised until other dimensions of the IT business case have been addressed. For example to produce a convincing macro model it is necessary to have performed a strategic alignment check. To be able to produce the detailed costing required for the micro model it is necessary to have performed at least some of the work required for the technology statement. Thus in an important sense the different elements of the IT business case are contingent upon each other.

	Macro model	**Details**
1.1	Name of the proposed intervention	*Electronic credit control system*
1.2	State the perceived problem or opportunity	*There has been a steady deterioration in the performance of the credit control activities of the organisation. Whereas the average rate of bad debts was 0.025% during the 1980s the rate during the 1990s has been 0.040%. In addition the average number of days in debtors during the 1980s was 35 and this number has increased during the 1990s to 47 days. There are no doubt several reasons for this including the tough economic and financial climate generally experienced during the 1990s.*
1.3	Why is it a problem or opportunity	*Credit control activities have not been given as much attention in recent years as perhaps they should have been. As a result of a benchmarking exercise it is now established that the industry average for bad debts is 0.02% and the average number of days in debtors in the industry is 40.*
1.4	What is the nature of the intervention	*To establish an electronic link to the local credit rating operators.* *To provide an on-line interface between the sales order processing activities and the billing and debtors activities which will highlight if a particular client is about to be given further credit when their account is overdue or over their credit limit.* *To make on-line reports available to credit chasers to ensure that payment is made within the agreed number of days.*
1.5	What will be the result of the intervention?	*The organisation's credit control activities will be brought into line with the industry averages.* *The outcome of the new sales and credit process will be an improvement in profit and cash flow, which will produce a payback of less than one year and an ROI of 120%*
1.6	Identify the owner-users	*Chief accountant, Credit controller, Sales manager, Credit rating controllers, Credit chasers*
1.7	State the time frame required	*This needs to be achieved within a six-month period.*

Figure 4.4: The macro model form after completion

The information that will be collected by completing the seven parts of the macro model form will constitute the text of the model. As well as producing the macro model in words it is also useful to describe the by means of a diagram and an example of this can be seen in Figure 4.4.

4.2.2   Example of a macro model for credit control process

The following is an example of a macro model that has been developed to describe a requirement for a credit control and administration system. The macro model is initially presented in the detailed format described in Figure 4.3 and then subsequently as an integrated whole. The macro model form is simply a checklist which assisted the modeller ensure that all the main issues have been addressed.

Integrating the information in the macro model form will produce the high level description of the proposed intervention and it outcomes together with the stakeholders, timeframe, etc. This will appear as shown in Figure 4.5.

There has been a steady deterioration in the performance of the credit control activities of the organisation. Whereas the average rate of bad debts was 0.025% during the 1980s the rate during the 1990s has been 0.040%. In addition the average number of days in debtors during the 1980s was 35 and this number has increased during the 1990s to 47 days. There are no doubt several reasons for this including the tough economic and financial climate generally experienced during the 1990s.

It is also true to say that the credit control activities have not been given as much attention in recent years as perhaps they should have been. As a result of a benchmarking exercise it is now established that the industry average for bad debts is 0.02% and the average number of days in debtors in the industry is 40. It is now considered necessary to take action to bring the organisation's experience in this respect into line with the industry averages and then to improve on its performance in this respect again from that position.

It has been decided that the chief accountant takes direct responsibility for the credit control activities and work on new systems in collaboration with the credit controller and the sales manager. Together these individuals will implement a credit control system that will identify potential bad debts before a sale is made so that an insightful decision can be made as to whether or not to do business with the potential client.

4.3 Example of the macro model for a sales administration system

Establishing an electronic link to the local credit rating operators will do this. In addition there will be an on-line interface between the sales order processing activities and the billing and debtors activities which will highlight if a particular client is about to be given further credit when their account is overdue or over their credit limit. Furthermore on-line reports will be made available to credit chasers to ensure that payment is made within the agreed number of days. The outcome of the new sales and credit process will be an improvement in profit and cash flow, which will produce a payback of less than one year and an ROI of 120%. This needs to be achieved within a six-month period.

Figure 4.5 An integrated high level macro model

The macro model can also be represented diagrammatically to help clarify the key stages required. Figure 4.6 identifies the problem the system is to solve as described in Figure 4.4 and Figure 4.7 describes the proposed system as described in Figure 4.5.

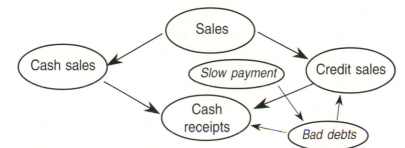

Figure 4.6 Diagrammatic view of the problem

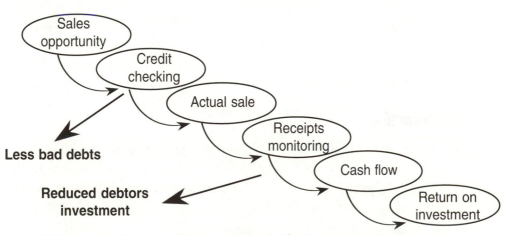

Figure 4.7 Diagrammatic view of the macro model for the proposed system

4.3 Example of the macro model for a sales administration system

The following is an example of a macro model that is expressed in words only. This model describes the business problem, it suggests a solution and it explains how the solution will solve the problem.

Average gross sales invoice values are generally too small to provide the required return on investment. If the average gross sales invoice value is increased by a factor of five, then the cost of administration will come into line with the industry average and this will result in a higher profit and thus a satisfactory return on investment. The average gross sales invoice value may be increased by the more effective selection of clients as well as by a greater concentration on cross selling. Clients may be more effectively selected if the relevant sales persons have access to appropriate sales history and market potential information. Similarly, appropriate information systems may enhance the opportunity for cross selling by identifying potential needs for a wider range of our products in our already established client base.

Figure 4.8 Example of macro model expressed in words

The above statement qualifies as a model because:

◆ it is a clear description of a problem, a proposed process which is expected to improve the situation, and it suggests a likely result;

◆ it facilitates a discussion of the proposed intervention and possible alternative courses of action.

This macro model can also be expressed graphically. Figure 4.9 presents the written macro model statement above. This type of graphical model usually does not include much detail but rather the general issues that are involved and the direction in which the organisation intends to move.

4.4 Meso model

A meso model provides a half-way stage between the high level, overview of the macro model and the detailed financial statement which constitutes the micro model. Figures 4.10 and 4.11 are examples of meso models derived from the macro models for the credit control system and sales administration system described above.

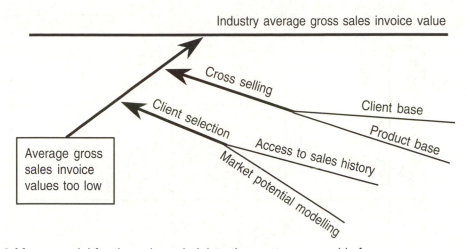

Figure 4.9 Macro model for the sales administration system – graphic form

An essential feature of a meso model is that all the possible benefits are listed and that each benefit has a specific metric matched with it. Benefits that do not have a suitable metric should not be listed. It is the meso model that provides the raw material from which the micro model will ultimately be produced.

For benefits to be achieved they need to be in some way measurable i.e. a stakeholder should be able to assess whether they have been delivered. Thus it is necessary to establish metrics that can be associated with any benefits that have been specified as possibly stemming from the information systems investment. This will allow an objective assessment to be made as to the extent to which the information system has delivered the benefits.

The primary benefits of some systems will essentially be simple functional requirements that will either exist or not exist. Such benefits will be evaluated on a yes/no binary scale. Others will be qualitative benefits that can only be evaluated on a qualitative scale (very good, good, satisfactory, poor, very poor). Finally some benefits will be measurable on an agreed numeric scale. For example, 'average invoice value' can be measured on a '£ per Invoice' scale and a target set to define a satisfactory business benefit resulting from the information system development project.

4.4 Meso model

Output	Business outcome	Specific benefits	Measurement method	Specific metric	Responsibility	Time frame
Credit history of prospective client	Better return on the firm's sales efforts	Less bad debts	Reduction in accounts handed over for collection and less write off	Number of interactions with lawyers, lower legal fees, less bad debts	Credit controller	Three months from start of project
Reports on law suits	Protection of profit margins	Less bad debts	Reduction in accounts handed over for collection and less write off	Number of interactions with lawyers, lower legal fees. less bad debts	Sales manager	Four months from start of project
Monthly receipts report	Collect cash and slow down or stop credit to doubtful debtors	Faster cash flow, more interest earned at bank, more supplier discounts available, less bad debts	Cash balance. lower cost of purchases, reduction in accounts handed over for collection and less write off	Cash, profit, etc	Chief accountant, credit controller, sales manager	Six months from start of project

Figure 4.10 Meso Model for the credit control system

Output	Business outcome	Specific benefits	Measurement method	Specific metric	Responsi-bility	Time frame
Reports on sales per client	Better return on the firm's sales efforts	Better customer service	Customer satisfaction surveys (1) Distributed questionnaires	SERVQUAL Determination of expected service and the service which the customer perceives	Sales manager	6 mths
			(2) Personal interviews	Qualitative data to be analysed using interpretative techniques		
Unfulfilled orders reports	Forecast clients' requirements	Better utilisation of inventory	Inventory and sales statistics	Inventory turnover. Number of days' sales in inventory	Corporate planner	6 mths
Vehicle tracking reports	Improve utilisation of corporate assets	Better employment of transport fleet	Vehicle tracking system	Petrol consumption	Commercial manager	3 mths
			Matching vehicles to customer orders	Number of deliveries per day. Number of vehicles on the road vs. number of deliveries		
Speed of servicing of client complaints	Better utilisation of corporate resources	Better job satisfaction of personnel from sales administration	Staff satisfaction survey	Gap between expectations and performance	Sales administrator	6 mths
Cost reports	Lower cost profile	Lower administrative costs	Accounting system	Cost per invoice/credit note, etc.	Accountants	6 mths

Figure 4.11 Meso model for the sales administration system

4.5 How to develop a meso model

In developing the meso model the following questions need to be asked and satisfactory answers need to be found.

1 Which specific changes to procedures or practices will be initiated by the IT investment?

2 How will these changes affect a specific business result.

3 How will these business results be measured?

4 What metric will be used in this measurement process?

5 Who will be responsible for ensuring that the IT investment will produce the required output and outcome?

6 In what time frame are these outcomes required?

These questions are best answered by the principal stakeholders, who may wish to negotiate how some of these matters will be managed. It is important that these type of questions are not simply left to IT professionals, for although they need to provide input here, it should be the users/owners who have the loudest say in matters such as these. Chapter 5 discusses the issue of the principal stakeholders.

It may not be a simple matter to produce a convincing meso model. Some of the outcomes may produce intangible benefits and these do present challenges from the point of view of the measurement and metric issues. However there are several different approaches to quantifying benefits and in the case of the meso model it is not necessary to only rely on financial quantification of benefits. Therefore in the meso model a metric such as *ServeQual*, (Parasuraman *et al.* 1985) which has been adapted to measure user satisfaction may be employed (Remenyi *et al.* 1997). Other measures may be statistics with regard to the number of new clients or an increase in the length of service of staff, etc.

4.6 Generic categories of IT benefit

There are two generic categories of IT benefit which can be referred to as *tangible* and *intangible*.

A tangible IT benefit is one which directly affects the firm's profitability, whereas an intangible IT benefit is one which can be seen to have a positive effect on the firm's business, but does not necessarily directly influence the firm's profitability.

Within the broad categories of tangible and intangible benefits a further classification is required as different types of benefit may be *quantifiable* or *unquantifiable*.

A quantifiable tangible IT benefit is one which directly affects the firm's profitability and the effect of which is such that it may be objectively measured, for example, reduction in costs or assets or an increase in revenue. An unquantifiable tangible IT benefit can also be seen to directly affect the firm's profitability, but the precise *extent* to which it does cannot be directly measured. Examples include the ability to obtain better information through the use of IT, improving the corporate risk profile and improving the firm's security.

Intangible benefits can also be sub-classified in the same way. A quantifiable intangible IT benefit is one which can be measured, but its impact does not necessarily directly affect the firm's profitability. For example, obtaining information faster, providing better customer satisfaction or improved staff satisfaction. Perhaps the most difficult type of IT benefit is the unquantifiable intangible benefit. This refers to benefits that cannot easily be measured and the impact of the benefit does not necessarily directly affect the firm's profitability. Examples include improved market reaction to the firm, customer perception or potential employees' perception to the firm's product.

These different types of generic IT benefits can be illustrated in a 2 x 2 matrix as shown in Figure 4.12.

The different benefit types described above can be measured using specific measuring techniques. These are shown in Figure 4.13.

There are several different types of cost-benefit analysis that can be used to measure the effect of staff reductions, lower assets or more sales in financial terms. The techniques are discussed in Chapter 9.

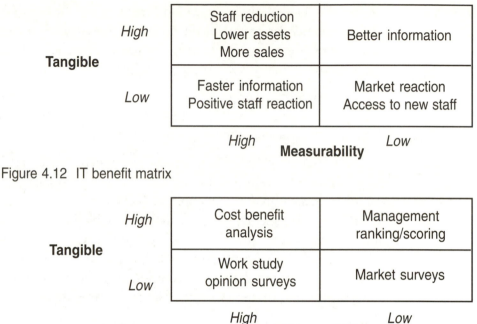

Figure 4.12 IT benefit matrix

Figure 4.13 Benefit measurement techniques

It is generally believed that cost-benefit analysis provides *hard* measures while the other measures are *soft*. In effect, although cost-benefit analysis is always reduced to monetary terms it is not always as hard as it appears.

From the point of view of preparing the meso model it is not difficult to include tangible benefits and describe them in the seven different columns provided in Figure 4.9. The intangible benefits offer a greater challenge, as it will be necessary to decide which type of measuring approaches to use and what an appropriate metric would look like.

4.7 Micro model

A micro model is usually presented as a detailed financial representation of how the project will proceed, in which the set-up costs, the on-going cost, the on-going benefits and the net benefits are specifically stated. The micro model should also include the investment statistics that are commonly used by organisations for their general capital investment appraisals. These performance statistics might include paybacks, return on investment, net present value, internal rate of return and profitability index. These are the sort of measures where were referred to by Peter Drucker (1988) and quoted in Chapter 1.

The detailed or micro model takes the issues described in more general business terms in the meso model and attempts to quantify them in financial terms. This quantification will usually be undertaken in terms of financial estimates of the costs and the benefits.

The micro model described in Figure 4.14 associates financial values to a generic IT investment.

Cost displacement statement	£'000
Investment costs	
Hardware	19000
Software	2200
Communications	750
Commissioning	150
Total start up cost	5000
On-going costs	
Maintenance	300
People	150
Consumables	120
Accommodation	50
Total operating expenses	620
Estimated benefits	
Staff no longer required	950
Office expenses	450
Reduction in finacne charges due to capital release	550
Total	1950
Net benefit	1330
ROI	26%
Payback	4 years

Figure 4.14: A micro model showing cost-benefit analysis

Figure 4.14 shows only one scenario. In fact it is usual to develop more than one such view of the IT investment as well as perhaps what-if analysis or even sensitivity analysis.

Chapter 9 deals with the micro model in more detail. However it should be mentioned here that in respect to developing this model it is most important to use marginal costs only, and not to attempt to include all the so-called hidden costs, i.e. not the full range of ownership costs. Care needs to be taken to produce the micro model for an appropriate time horizon. Also as the numbers in the micro model are only estimates, it is essential not to become involved in spurious accuracy and detail. It is useful to remember to test each line in the micro model for materiality[3] and credibility.

4.8 Summary

An outcome statement is at the heart of a professionally produced business case for an IT investment. In fact some IT practitioners and consultants regard the outcome statement as the single most important part of the IT business case. The development of outcome statements is essential for the maximisation of IT investment effectiveness. Without outcome and associated benefit statements the best that can be hoped for is an unclear view of what the IT investment may achieve and how this will actually take place. To ensure that there is a clear understanding of how the IT investment will proceed and how the outcome and associated benefits will be generated it is essential to develop macro, meso and micro models, i.e. at all the three levels described in this chapter.

The outcome statements are regarded by many as the cornerstone on which the rest of the IT investment business case is built.

Forms which may be used to help produce the deliverables required from this phase of the business case are shown in Appendix A.

---

[3] The materiality test implies that very small amounts of costs need not be included in the micro model and that only the substantial cost items are really important. Of course it is sometimes quite difficult to know where this point of materiality actually starts.

5 **The stakeholders**

In a time of drastic change it is the learners who inherit the future. The learned usually find themselves equipped to live in a world that no longer exists.

Eric Hoffer, *Reflections on the Human Condition* (1973)

Here is Edward Bear, coming downstairs now, bump, bump, bump, on the back of his head, behind Christopher Robin. It is, as far as he knows, the only way of coming downstairs, but sometimes he feels that there is another way, if only he could stop bumping for a moment and think of it.

A.A Milne, *Winnie-the-Pooh* (1926)

5.1   Introduction

Stakeholder knowledge and management is central to the preparation of a comprehensive IT investment business case. It is also central to the management of the IT project itself.

Knowing and understanding the requirements and motivation of the IT investment stakeholders is a critical part of preparing a business case for that investment. To achieve this it is important to be able to identify the relevant stakeholders, pressure groups and other interested parties and to assess their interests in terms of how they will react to the change brought about by the intervention or project. This is because if the principal stakeholders are not satisfied, the information system will be regarded as a failure. This view is supported by Oz who pointed out:

If the aggregate expectation of stakeholders from the IS is not met, the organisation is facing an expectation failure. (Oz 1994)

In fact stakeholders and their expectations are so important that Lyytinen has pointed out that:

... an IS failure [is] a gap between stakeholders' expectations expressed in some ideal or standard and the actual performance. (Lyytinen 1987)

It is important to clarify what is meant by the term stakeholder. According to Svendsen:

The term 'stakeholders' refers to the individual or groups who can affect or be affected by a corporation's activities. (Svendsen 1998)

In the context of this book an IT investment stakeholder is defined as any individual or group with an involvement in the project interested in improving the business processes or practices being supported by the proposed IT investment. This can include senior management, users/owners, IT professionals, financial managers and administrators, vendors, trade unions, as well as a variety of other individuals and groups.

Thus an IT investment project can have a substantial number of different stakeholders, and one of the challenges is to manage the contributions from a number of different interested parties.

5.2   The importance of stakeholders

During the past few years increasing attention has been given to the issue of stakeholders, not only in IT matters but in corporate affairs generally. There are a number of reasons for this, including the fact that concern for stakeholders is now regarded as good for business practice, especially in the longer term. Svendsen (1998) has succinctly expressed this when she said:

Today, companies are investing in longer-term relationships.

In fact she went on to say that:

Positive stakeholders relationships can also affect profitability indirectly because intangibles like trusting relationships with suppliers, employees' capacity for learning and growth, and a company's reputation and goodwill are key drivers of corporate competitiveness and profitability. (Svendsen 1998)

Stakeholders concern means that the organisation is aware of the fact that its behaviour has a direct impact on the greater community in which it exists. In the IT investment context, stakeholders concern amounts to the fact that the organisation realises that the IT professional alone cannot ensure the success of an IT investment. It requires a team effort in which the IT profession is only one player. The actual number of stakeholders will vary from organisation to organisation and from application to application but there will inevitable be considerably more people involved than just the group of IT professionals.

5.3   The IT stakeholder

Increasingly, it is being realised that a positive stakeholder relationship is a *sine qua non* for IT investment success. The presence of a constructive relationship between the key players in the IT project make a big difference between success and failure. In the past, stakeholder relationships were generally not regarded as that important, except perhaps from the point of view of controlling the scope of the project. However today this attitude has for many organisations, changed. Stakeholder relationships before, during, and after an IT project is commissioned, are seen as central issues. These relationships, however need to be collaborative and dynamic and this is well expressed by Svendsen when she said:

A collaborative approach to building stakeholders relationships, on the other hand, sees the stakeholders relationships as being reciprocal, evolving, and mutually defined. (Svendsen 1998)

The importance of stakeholder relationships is such that if for any reason the stakeholders are in conflict, the probability of IT project success is significantly reduced. Stakeholder relationships require trust and co-operation from all the parties concerned and this can be difficult to achieve. However, when these relationships are positive it can produce a distinctly significant competitive advantage.

5.4   The three major groups of stakeholders

Although in the IT investment context there could be many different types of stakeholders, it is useful to discuss them in terms of three major categories. These principal or primary stakeholder categories are the users/owners, the IT professionals and the finance and administration staff. However over and above these three groups of stakeholders, top management will often be an important over-riding stakeholder. This is partly because the investment in the new processes which require the IT support may both be very expensive and also because the type of changes required do sometimes go to the very heart of the business.

5.5   The users/owners as stakeholders

Users/owners are probably the most important set of principal stakeholders of any proposed system. The users/owners are likely to have the most influence in making the business process supported by the IT investment a success. This group will make intensive use of the information systems when they have been developed. The users/owners group needs to include individuals from various levels within the organisation. This means that it is important to obtain the backing of both senior users/owner managers, as well as the individuals who will routinely use the new processes and systems.

There may also be a number of other users who will work with the system from time to time and thus have an interest in the way the project is conceived and developed, but who may not be regarded as primary stakeholders. One of the tasks of the project manger will be to decide how to represent the interests of these stakeholders. It is important that they are not ignored or forgotten. Figure 5.1 is a checklist of users/owners stakeholders.

Users/owners
- ❑ Top managers
- ❑ Senior managers
- ❑ Middle managers
- ❑ Supervisors
- ❑ Operatives
- ❑ Trade union representatives
- ❑ Clients or customers
- ❑ Suppliers

Figure 5.1: The major sub-groups within the user/owner stakeholders

Ideally the users/owners should be responsible for the development of the IT investment business case. They should be the primary motivators for the investment. The users/owners need to play a key role in the management of the IT development project and should be the arbitrators of whether or not the IT investment has succeeded. This is a large role for the users/owners, who may not be adequately skilled to be able to perform all these functions well and therefore will frequently need to be supported by the other principal stakeholders.

5.6 IT professionals as stakeholders

The group of IT professionals who will work with the technical development of the information systems are clearly stakeholders of some considerable importance. They supply the IT expertise which will make the technology aspects of the new processes work. Traditionally in-house IT professionals have accepted a large part of the responsibility for the success of the IT investment. It was not uncommon for IT professionals to develop information systems for their so-called end-users. Sometimes this was done without adequate consultation, as IT professionals have been known to believe that they knew what the user requirements were, at least as well as the users themselves. Clearly this was not very satisfactory as there has been problems of communications between IT professionals and users, as well as the development of what is sometimes referred to as the culture gap. Increasingly it is thought that the users/owners need to play a greater role in ensuring the success of the IT investment.

However the IT professional still has a totally indispensable role to play in any IT investment project. The IT professional should be seen as a critical adviser to the users/owners who will ensure that the appropriate technology is acquired and employed. The role of the IT professional has also been complicated by the fact that some organisations have outsourced the supply of IT expertise.

Outsourcing has been a familiar aspect of the supply of IT competencies in many organisations over the past years. Few organisations have never used contractors or from time to time employed consultants. However it has only been in recent years that organisations have outsourced all, or the major part of the IT operation. Today organisations increasingly use a portfolio of IT expertise, which includes both internal and external people and organisations. These sources of IT expertise are shown in Figure 5.2.

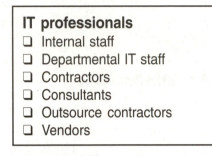

Figure 5.2: The more usual sources of IT expertise

Usually several of these groups are involved as stakeholders in an IT investment.

5.7 Financial managers and administrators as stakeholders

The third group of principal or primary stakeholders is the financial managers and administrators. Financial managers and administrators are always stakeholders in any corporate investment as they are instrumental in making the funds available for the purchase of the equipment, etc. Financial managers and administrators will arrange the contracts and ensure that goods are received and that payments are made, etc.

Financial managers and administrators are often involved with the detail of the business case accounting, as users/owners may not be familiar with the costing approaches required. IT investments which are made to improve business processes and practices will often affect the internal controls within the organisation, and for that reason both internal and external auditors may be required to advise on the propriety of the new proposals.

Investments often have to be audited and this will require further involvement from auditors.

Figure 5.3 lists some of the stakeholders that fall into this category.

Financial services
- ❑ Financial managers
- ❑ Accountants
- ❑ Capital budgeting staff
- ❑ Corporate treasury staff
- ❑ Corporate planners
- ❑ Corporate strategists
- ❑ Internal auditor
- ❑ External auditors
- ❑ Buyers

Figure 5.3: Some of the financial managers and administrator stakeholders

5.8 Different stakeholders – different views

There will always be a substantial number of different stakeholders associated with an IT investment. All IT investments are people-dependent and the preparation of the IT business case is highly dependent on the views of the different people, i.e. the different stakeholders. People produce these IT business cases and it is always some individual person's work or department or territory, in some form, that is being considered for change.

Furthermore, it is people who will make assumptions and predictions about IT value and worth, who will assemble business cases. In IT business case development the role of the evaluator is sometimes suggested to be neutral. The IT business case developer attempts, it is said, to make the evaluation event impersonal by using an objective method and objective data to measure the value and contribution of the IT. This is irrespective of whether an ex-ante or ex-post, or a summative or formative evaluation is being conducted. Of course this has not always been the case as it is nearly impossible to be neutral in the assessment of corporate investments. In fact an

IT investment business case should not be a neutral statement, but rather a statement of what the stakeholders are prepared to commit themselves to in terms of the proposed new processes and practices. Thus it is essential to remember that the IT business case is purposeful and is carried out to a particular end. The stakeholders interpret the value of the system in their terms, and their view of the particular situation is subject to human values and behaviour. This is identified by Walsham (1993) who states that there are a 'multiplicity of private rationalities' that influence the IT business case. It is important for the individuals whose systems are being studied to know and to accept the criteria that are being used in the IT business case. Unfortunately there are no common or universally agreed standards or scales for interpreting the value of IT holistically or even of evaluating individual measurable aspects of an IT investment. This view is supported by Lacity and Hirschheim when they said:

The problem is that meaningful measures of departmental efficiency do not exist for IS. (Lacity and Hirschheim 1995)

It is perhaps for this reason that the IT business case needs to be driven by all the principal stakeholders. The principal stakeholders should really know what is involved and will be able to lead the organisation into using the IT investment in the most suitable manner so that an appropriate return will be achieved on the investment.

However each group of stakeholders will have different views about the IT investment and it will be necessary to resolve these differences as much as possible. This will usually take the form of negotiations over the scope of the IT project. Typically the users/owners will want the scope to be as wide as possible and the IT professionals will want to confine the scope to a level they find to be relatively easily achievable. The financial managers and administrators will have their eye on the cost and the return on investment as well as how the new process will impact internal controls. Figure 5.4 shows how the negotiation among the three groups of stakeholders will involve feedback loops as they attempt to reach consensus about the scope of the IT investment. In this context participation from a wide range of individuals in the development of the IT business case is an important issue. It is not adequate to leave this process to senior managers, who may be distant from the proposed new processes, as this will produce a distorted view of how the IT investment will actually work.

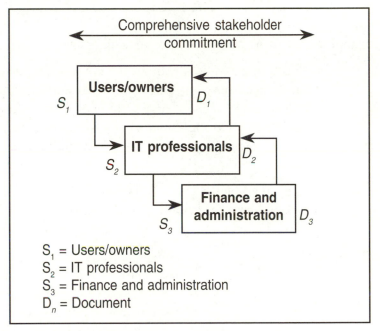

Figure 5.4: Feedback loops between the groups of prinicapl stakeholders

5.9 Stakeholders – for and against

Some stakeholders may be in favour of the IT investment while others may not. Thus to ensure the success of an IT project, it is essential to understand not only who the stakeholders are, but also what their attitudes to the project are.

As well as dividing stakeholders into those who are in favour of the IT investment and those who are against it may also be viewed in terms of how active or passive they are. Using the two dimensions of in favour and against and active and passive, a 2 x 2 matrix may be developed as shown in Figure 5.5.

5.9 Stakeholders – for and against

Stakeholders

	In favour	Against
Active	Fans	Old defenders
Passive	Sleeping partners	Sleeping dogs

Figure 5.5: Dimensions of stakeholder involvement

Ideally stakeholders should be active promoters or supporters of the project, have an interest in the results, and be involved in the management of the changes brought about by the project. On the other hand stakeholders may not be active at all, but rather play a passive role and thus have no real influence on the project at all.

Of course sometimes stakeholders may not be supportive and in fact sometimes they may be antagonistic to the project. In any event stakeholders can usually influence a situation, and project managers will need to be able to acquire and retain their support or minimise their antagonism wherever possible.

It is important to have as many of the different stakeholders in the fans quadrant. However, if they are not in that quadrant it is important to try to prevent them from taking a position in the old defenders quadrant if possible. The stakeholders in the old defenders quadrant will actively resist the project as they see it as a threat to their current position.

Of course the position of stakeholders does not remain static and a stakeholder who is a fan, if not handled correctly, may become an opponent or an old defender. It is for this reason that stakeholder management is critical to the success of a project.

A stakeholder management programme should have as an objective to move the sleeping partners up into the top left-hand quadrant where they would become a fan. Similarly the stakeholder management programme should attempt to move the old defenders down into the bottom right-hand quadrant where they would become one of the sleeping dogs. This is illustrated in Figure 5.6.

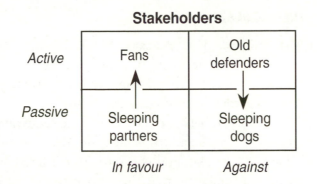

Figure 5.6: Changing the dimensions of stakeholder involvement

5.10 Stakeholder management

The IT investment business case may be seen as the platform from which a sound programme of project management can be launched. To achieve this it is necessary be able to manage the stakeholder situation. Thus it is important for the project managers be able to:

1 Identify the relevant stakeholders, pressure groups and other interested parties;

2 Assess stakeholder interests in terms of how they will react to the change brought about by the project;

3 Assess stakeholder commitment or antagonism;

4 Assess stakeholder power to promote or hinder the success of the project.

This information is required in order to evaluate stakeholder relations and ensure continued support, as well as to minimise any opposition from the stakeholders.

5.10.1 Identifying stakeholders

When embarking on a large-scale project it is important to itemise the range of activities that will be involved and to identify exactly who the players or actors in the project will be, together with their roles. This is a way of creating a comprehensive list or map of all the principal stakeholders in the project.

5.10.2 The stakeholder map

A stakeholder map is created by placing on a sheet of paper the name of the project that is being contemplated and then drawing circles around the sheet, each circle identifying an individual or group regarded as having a stake in the project. Place the most significant individuals or groups nearer the centre and other less significant individuals or groups around the edge. Have all the stakeholders named in this map and check to see if there have been any omissions, thus ensuring that the map includes all relevant interests, including: senior management, colleagues, staff, people in other organisations. Figure 5.7 is an example of a stakeholder (S/H) map.

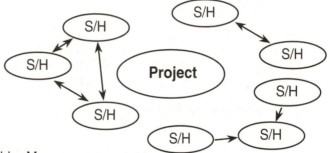

Figure 5.7: Stakeholder Map

Note that the way different stakeholders and stakeholder groups relate to each other may directly affect the project. These types of relationships can be indicated on the stakeholder map by interconnecting lines or by the absence of these interconnecting lines. For example, lines which show arrows at both end may be used to represent complex two-way relationships where both groups of stakeholders may influence one another. If the arrow has only one head then the relationship is only one way with the second stakeholders being influenced but not being able to exert any counter influence. Where stakeholders are unconnected then they are "stand alone" stakeholders who do not influence anyone else.

This type of map can also be used to show how relationships between stakeholders may change during the project. For example, during the course of the project, the reactions of different stakeholder groups may affect the attitudes of others. Concessions given to one group can quite likely affect the expectations of others. This could be shown on the stakeholder map.

5.10.3 Assess stakeholder commitment

Using a stakeholder commitment assessment table such as the one shown in Figure 5.8, details of the individual key stakeholders can be entered, and an assessment can be made as to what level of commitment each has towards the project. Figure 5.8 shows some example entries, where an *x* has be placed in the column that best fits the current commitment of a particular stakeholder and a *y* has been entered in the column that corresponds to the level of commitment that is considered adequate.

Key stakeholders	Strongly against	Against	Indifferent	Passively in favour	Actively in favour	Strongly in favour
Capital budgeting officers			*x*		*y*	
Internal IT					*x*	*y*
User group						*x,y*

Figure 5.8: Stakeholder commitment assessment table

The stakeholder commitment assessment table is a useful device for clarifying the position of each stakeholder group and it may also be used to discuss with each group where they are and how they could be encouraged to move to a more positive position.

5.10.4 Analysis of stakeholder power

To be able to manage the stakeholders it is important to perform an analysis of their positions and the type of power they may be able to exert. To do this it is necessary to establish:

1 Who is the project sponsor?

2 Who is the project champion?

3 Who is the key project manager?

4 Who will own the project?

5 Who has most to lose if the project succeeds?

6 Who has most to gain from the project?

7 Whose attitude do you most want to change?

8 What capacity does each stakeholder have to help or hinder the project?

9 Which stakeholder should you most concentrate your efforts on?

5.10.5 Assess stakeholder interests

The stakeholder interests and action assessment is another helpful device in the management of the stakeholders. This assessment can be used to enter the key stakeholders and then to record the answers to the following six questions for each stakeholder group. Finding answers to these questions can be challenging, but they are critical to ensuring the success of the project.

1 What are the priorities, goals, and interests of each group of stakeholders?

2 How have they been involved in similar past projects and how might this information be useful with regard to possible reactions during this project?

3 What specific input is required of them during the project, e.g. active intervention on specific tasks, ability to work in a new job?

4 What are the possible benefits for each group of stakeholders?

5 What are their expectations from the project and what is their attitude to it?

6 What is their likely reaction to this IT investment opportunity and what issues or questions might they raise?

Figure 5.9 is an example assessment of how the capital budget stakeholder group might respond to the questions.

By performing a stakeholder interests and action assessment it should be possible to decide how the stakeholders can be influenced to support the project by identifying which project benefits will add value to each group of stakeholders.

Stakeholder group: *Capital budgeting officers*	
1	What are the priorities, goals, and interests of this group? *To ensure that a realistic budget is provided for the IT investment and that any changes to the detail of the budget are closely monitored throughout the project.*
2	How has this group been involved in similar past projects and how might this information be useful with regard to possible reactions during this project? *This group of stakeholders have traditionally been cautious of estimates of spend provided by Internal IT and thus further cost-benefit analysis should be considered.*
3.	What specific input is required of this group during the project, e.g. active intervention on specific tasks, ability to work in a new job? *The capital budget group should be prepared to re-evaluate expenditure periodically throughout the project.*
4	What are the possible benefits for this group of stakeholders? *Continuous participation of the capital budget group can ensure closer adherence to budget estimates.*
5	What are the expectations of this group from the project and what is their attitude to it? *The capital budget group is relatively indifferent to this specific project as it is one of several investment programmes they are currently involved with. Their expectations at this stage are that the project will probably exceed its budget and take longer than the estimated time.*
6	What is the likely reaction of this group to this IT investment opportunity and what issues or questions might they raise? *The capital budget group will usually be conservative and will question the viability of the proposal, especially insofar as its ability to earn a suitable return on investment is concerned. This group of stakeholders will probably call for detailed justification of all the cost and benefit items within the business case accounting statement.*

Figure 5.9: Example stakeholder interests and action assessment

5.11 The stakeholders and the IT business case

From Figure 2.4 on page 25 it may be seen that stakeholders are involved in the IT business case in at least two distinct senses.

In the first instance when the business process or practice improvement opportunity is first raised it is necessary to establish an individual or group of individuals who will propose the project or intervention. Clearly it is very much better if these are stakeholders and ideally principal or primary stakeholders such as the users/owners. But there will always be more than one group of stakeholders and thus the stakeholder issue needs to be addressed again within the IT business case by establishing who is likely to be for and against the IT investment and how these views may be managed. This is regarded by many as perhaps one of the greatest challenges which needs to be faced if the IT project is to succeed.

Of course the IT investment business case will ultimately need to be approved and once again the question of which stakeholders are most involved at this stage is a central issue. If possible a widely representative group of stakeholders should be involved at this stage as this tends to support later commitment to the IT project. It is certainly important that top management or IT management does not push IT projects which do not have wide support from the primary stakeholders.

5.12 Summary

There can be many stakeholders involved in projects that change business processes and practices. In this chapter three major groups of primary stakeholders are described. However in addition to these primary stakeholders, top management has always to be regarded as supremely important, if not overriding stakeholder.

It is important to understand that not all stakeholders may be sympathetic to the IT project and care needs to be given to the management of anyone who may not be supportive of the project. Stakeholders are actually all-important to the success of an IT project. It is therefore essential that the stakeholders be on side right from the very start of the IT investment.

It is critically important to the success of a project that top management or IT management does not push IT projects which do not have wide support from the primary stakeholders.

6 | Strategic alignment and IT benefit identification

Strategy can be defined as the determination of the basic long-term goals and objectives of an enterprise, and the adoption of courses of action and the allocation of resources necessary for carrying out these goals.

(Chandler 1990)

Strategy pertains to a firm's plan of action that causes it to allocate its scarce resources over time to get from where it is to where it wants to go.

(Pascale 1986)

6.1 Introduction

The organisation's corporate strategy is of central importance to the effective use of IT. Strategic mismatches are a major cause of IT project failure and care needs to be taken not to fall into a trap whereby the IT investment is pulling the organisation in a different way to the overall corporate strategy. Thus the question of IT alignment is a critical aspect of the development of an IT investment business case. However the issues related to corporate strategy are not always well understood, either by users/owners or by IT practitioners. Furthermore in some organisations it is not always clear precisely what their corporate strategy is.

Having established a corporate strategy, the IT investment business case then requires the specific benefits expected from the IT investment to be listed. When this is done an assessment cam be made as to whether these benefits support the strategy or not.

6.2 Strategy? What strategy?

Before discussing the issue of strategic alignment it is important to understand the concept of strategy.

6.2 Strategy? What strategy?

It is not a simple matter to define strategy. The problem is that there are many definitions of corporate strategy. Mintzburg *et al.* (1998) describes 10 schools of thought on the subject of corporate strategy with considerably more than 10 definitions. As was pointed out by Ansoff:

All firms have a strategy. Some firms spend much time and money in reducing their strategy to writing, while other simply act out their strategy and do not bother to articulate it. The former are said to have formulated their business strategy while the latter are said to have an implicit strategy. (Ansoff 1965)

Taking Ansoff's point further it is sometimes said that an organisation only needs an articulated corporate strategy when it has lost its original historic dynamic or raison d'être. Translated into practical terms this means that the strategy tells you what it is you are supposed to be doing! It is however most important to note that even firms who do not appear to have a corporate strategy actually do have an implicit strategy.

Another leading author in the field of corporate strategy offers a different dimension to the subject when he points out that he sees strategy as the master allocator. According to Quinn:

A strategy is the pattern or plan that integrates an organisation's major goals, policies and action sequences into a coherent whole. A well formed strategy helps to marshal and allocate an organisation's resources into a unique and viable posture based on its relative internal competencies and short-comings, anticipated changes in the environment, and contingent moves from intelligent opponents. (Quinn 1988)

It is also useful to understand where the focus of strategy should be placed. Ansoff points or that:

Strategic decisions are primarily concerned with external, rather than internal, problems of the firm and especially with selection of the product mix which the firm will produce and the markets to which it will sell. (Ansoff 1965)

And this is reinforced by Porter who said that:

The essence of formulating competitive strategy is relating a company to its environment. Although the relative environment is very broad, encompassing social as well as economic forces, the key aspects of the firm's environment is the industry or industries in which it competes. (Porter 1985)

Of course these definitions are incomplete without pointing out that strategy is also highly correlated with competencies. Thus Kay makes the point that:

The strategy of the firm is the match between its internal capabilities and its external relationships. It is how it responds to its suppliers, its customers, its competitors, and the social and economic environment in which it operates. The analysis of strategy uses our experience of the past to develop concepts, tools, data and models which will illustrate these decisions in the future. (Kay 1993)

Although these definitions of strategy provide distinct insights into what corporate strategy is and how it works in an organisation, it is not easy to operationalise these ideas and concepts. A more succinct and useful definition of corporate strategy in the IT investment environment is that:

Corporate strategy is how an organisation finds, gets and keeps it clients.

Accepting this as a functional definition of strategy means that it is relatively easy to see whether an IT investment supports the organisation's strategy. When it does, it is said that there is strategic alignment between the corporate strategy and the IT strategy.

6.3   Approaches to strategic thinking

To understand the ways in which an IT investment can be aligned with the organisation's corporate strategy it is necessary to review some of the more important corporate strategy models. There are many such models available, but the author has decided to restrict the discussion to models developed by Porter (1983, 1985) and Treacy and Wiersema (1993).

Although the origins of modern strategic thinking date back into the 1950s, the subject really began to gather momentum in the

1980's. Michael Porter is one of a small group of the most influential authors on the subject of corporate strategy and his work in this area may be best understood through three models that he proposed. These are the five forces model, the generic strategy model and the value chain model.

6.4 The five forces model

The model portrayed in Figure 6.1 illustrates Michael Porter's (1983,1985) five forces view of what determines an industry's attractiveness. It is maintained that a firm's performance is considerably confined by the five forces which act upon: the strength of the buyers and suppliers; the number of potential new entrants and substitutes available; and the rivalry among existing firms in the industry.

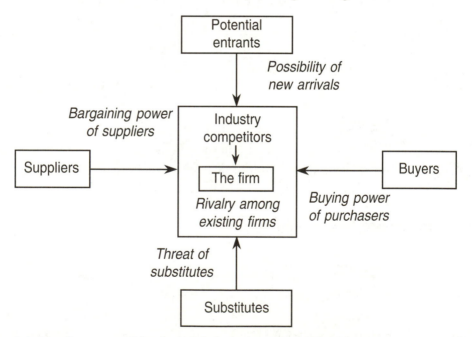

Figure 6.1: The five competitive forces in industry model (after Porter)

These five industry drivers or forces determine the relationship of the firm to its industry environment and this in turn is a major factor in establishing the organisation's opportunity to make profits and sustain reasonable growth levels. The five forces model explains why some industries are intrinsically highly profitable and others are not.

IT may be used to change the balance of power among the forces in the industry by techniques such as locking in clients and creating barriers to new entries, etc. If used correctly in this respect IT can either transform the business or alternatively can lead to the creation of new products, or even new ventures or enterprises.

IT may be used to strengthen relationships with buyers through systems such as those supplied to travel agents for reservations or printing of tickets. Relationships with suppliers may be strengthened through systems such as electronic data interchange (EDI). IT affects the way the organisation can fend off substitutes, improving the speed with which new and enhanced products are developed and marketed. Thus in this area, CAD and CAM systems are important. The home entertainment industry is an example of the use of IT in this way. In the area of potential entrants IT is sometimes used to increase the amount of funds an organisation needs to get started. The cost of airline reservation systems or banking ATMs is an example of this. With regards to rivalry among existing firms, here IT is used to promote the advantages of being a client of the organisation. Hotel reservation systems are an example of the use of IT in this way, especially Web or Intranet based systems.

6.5 Generic strategies model

The second Porter model described in Figure 6.2 focuses on the two generic strategies that a firm may adopt in its efforts to find and keep its clients.

Despite the fact that there are only two generic strategies, Figure 6.2 has four boxes. This is because these two generic strategies may be applied on a broad or narrow target basis. The only difference between broad target and narrow or niche approaches is the number of potential clients the firm is trying to reach, and thus the same types of IT are frequently applicable to both strategies.

Generic strategies for competitive advantage

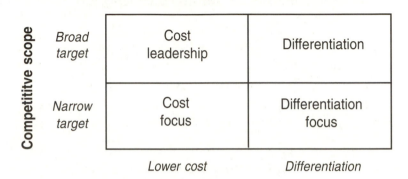

Figure 6.2: Generic strategy model (after Porter)

In this view a firm could enhance its market image and performance, and as a result obtain a premium price, or offer a low cost no frills product or service. By following one of these two generic strategies firms become superior performers in their industry. IT can be used to support either of these strategies by using access to data to enhance the product or service, or by using IT to contribute to a direct reduction in the firm's cost profile and thus the price for which the product or service is offered. Examples of using IT to differentiate the firm include remote purchasing systems, client support systems and field maintenance systems. Examples of the use of IT for cost reduction include flexible manufacturing systems, robotics, EDI, etc.

6.6   The value chain model

The third, value chain model, shown in Figure 6.3 provides a detailed view of the major organisational components comprising a typical business firm. This view argues that a strategy cannot be derived by considering the firm as a whole. It is suggested that a detailed analysis must be undertaken which will provide sufficient understanding of the business to be able to construct a suitable strategy. The value chain is Porter's tool or framework for carrying out the analysis.

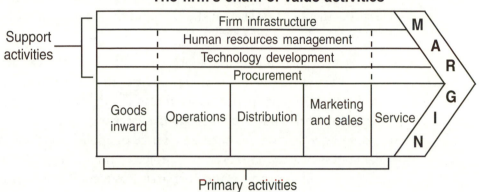

Figure 6.3: The value chain model (after Porter)

The value chain is described as the interrelationship of the value activities for the firm. Value activities divide the firm's operations into technologically and economically distinct activities that it must perform in order to do business. Therefore, by the nature of its business, its strategy and the industry in which it functions, firms will have distinctly different value activities and therefore distinctly different value chains.

6.6.1   Value activities

There are nine categories of value activity in a typical manufacturing firm. These are:

◆ Goods inwards

◆ Operations

◆ Distribution

◆ Marketing and sales

◆ Service

◆ Procurement

◆ Technological development

◆ Human resource management

◆ Firm's infrastructure

This value chain concept simply segments a firm into strategically relevant activities in order that the cost and the potential for differentiation can be examined.

IT investment plays a critical role in optimising both the efficiency and the effectiveness of all the value activities in the value chain. IT can improve corporate performance in each of the vertical, primary activities or horizontal support activities, sections. For example in the case of goods inwards there are a range of applications that can enhance this process. However, the choice of the most appropriate application will depend on the corporate strategy. If the organisation is pursuing a cost leadership strategy then the emphasis will need to be on how to minimise the IT expenditure and also how to apply IT to reduce other costs associated with the goods inwards function. If the organisation is pursuing a differentiation strategy then the emphasis will need to be on how to enhance the goods inwards function in such a way that the organisation can offer a better customer service. This could mean that there are more funds available for IT to support this function.

6.6.2   The industry value chain

As all firms may be seen to have value chains it is possible to also consider suppliers and customers value chains. Looked at as a whole, it is therefore also possible to consider the industry value chain. All the value activities of the members of the industry value chain represent a potential for competitive advantage and superior performance through both cost leadership and differentiation.

An important consequence of the value chain analysis is the notion that firms may link different elements of their own value chains to the value chains of other organisations in the industry. Figure 6.4 shows how a firm could link its operations to a buyer's distribution system, and its distribution (outbound logistics) to a client's goods inwards (inbound logistics). Firms could also make useful connections on the support activities level as well as between primary activities and support activities. Such links or joins will really only be effective through the use of IT, and show how a firm can take advantage of its industry value chain, as illustrated in Figure 6.4.

It is also possible for firms in different industry value chains to cooperate. This is usually referred to as establishing strategic alliances. In Figure 6.5, two industry value chains are shown, indicating how a strategic alliance may be set up. Firms that have successfully used IT in the above way have in numerous instances transformed their business, or given themselves very significant advantages in the marketplace. Key applications in this respect include inter-organisational systems (IOS) which may now be Web enhanced and perhaps leading to extranet type systems.

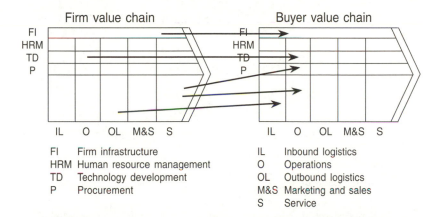

FI	Firm infrastructure
HRM	Human resource management
TD	Technology development
P	Procurement

IL	Inbound logistics
O	Operations
OL	Outbound logistics
M&S	Marketing and sales
S	Service

Figure 6.4: The industry value chain showing links between different organisations

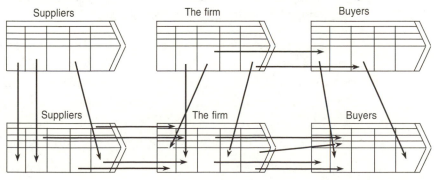

Figure 6.5: Industry value chain showing strategic alliances with suppliers, buyers, competitors, etc.

6.7 Strategy and the value package

Another approach to strategic formulation, as defined by Treacy and Wiersema (1993), considers the value package. According to this theory the best value package is centred on one of three approaches. As can be seen in Figure 6.6 there are three principal business systems available for delivering a best value package. These are to have the best product, to have the best total cost or to have the best total solution. As it is usually not possible to excel with all three systems, an organisation should focus on being a top performer in one business system and be on par with others in the market place on the other two value package approaches.

Figure 6.6: The three value propositions (after Treacy and Wiersema)

6.7.1 Operational excellence – Best total cost

To deliver a best value package through a best total cost system a firm will strive to deliver operational excellence. A firm adopting this system will usually apply a low price, but limited product variety strategy. A rigid approach to service needs to be applied. For this type of strategy to be successful there would need to be a lot of advertising, but little direct contact with the consumer.

To be successful along this strategic route the core processes or major challenges will include the need to:
◆ optimise the resource conversion process;

◆ facilitate end-to-end supply chain management;

◆ build sound partnerships within and without the firm

◆ be highly focused on efficiency, cost reduction and waste control and to apply process benchmarking.

The use of information technology for the operational excellence approach will require the organisation to focus on being highly automated for maximum efficiency. There will need to be much modelling and planning in order to optimise the resource conversion process. Mobile and remote technologies may be needed to integrate the internal value chain and to facilitate industry value optimisation. IS management is likely to be centralised with the emphasis on cost control and ROI, even in the short term. In the pursuit of operational excellence some systems could be outsourced.

Many retail organisations follow a strategy of best total cost and operational excellence.

6.7.2   Customer intimacy – Best total systems

To deliver a best value package through a best total system approach, a firm will pay much attention to customer intimacy. By this is meant that the firm must really understand its clients' business. The result of this will usually be the supply of technically sound products, tailored to the clients' requirements, but normally without much innovation. The expertise required by the firm attempting to follow the best total systems strategy reside in knowing the clients' exact needs and the ability to provide quick follow-up solutions to these needs with appropriate technology. Best total systems need be able to provide a tailored service with few glitches. The sales representatives will normally be responsible for ensuring the client gets what is required. This will usually result in the product being a little more expensive.

To be successful along this strategic route the core processes or major challenges will include the need for a basic win–win philosophy. The firm will need to put much emphasis on knowing in some detail, not only the client but also the market and the competition.

There needs to be a high level of flexibility in order to produce the product or service that the client really requires. Management needs be prepared to listen to the sales team and to the clients and to act upon the information.

The IT required to support this approach includes detailed customer databases and in-the-field sales/service systems. As the client is key to achieving a best total solution the firm needs be in a position to integrate its IT around the clients, supplying them with terminals where appropriate. There is likely to be less emphasis on short-term costs and there will probably be a longer-term view on ROI.

Vendors of large capital equipment often follow the strategy of best total systems and customer intimacy, as do firms of management and computer consultants.

6.7.3 Product leadership – Best product

To deliver a best value package through a product leadership strategy a firm will concentrate on producing the best product. This will require attention to the application of technology in order to innovate to produce a better product or service than the competition. Price is not a key issue when pursuing this strategy. Marketing will often be based on big bang launches.

To be successful along this route the core processes or major challenges will include the need for considerable investment in research and development to continually create high quality innovative products. Benchmarking will be important and firms must be prepared to discontinue products. In order to maintain product leadership it is important that new products get to the market quickly.

There will be a high reliance on IT. There must be a comprehensive set of tools to support research and development ranging from databases to CAD. Project management is likely to be supported by IT and it is not likely that systems will be outsourced.

Hi-tech organisations such as those in the electronics, aviation and pharmaceuticals industries frequently follow a product leadership strategy.

6.8 Specific IT applications and benefits

In order to be able to establish whether an IT investment is in alignment with the corporate strategy it is necessary to firstly identify the actual applications and the benefits the proposed new or enhanced process or practice supported by the IT investment is expected to deliver.

There are in fact a number of applications and benefits that new or enhanced processes or practices supported by the IT investment could produce. Sections 6.8.1 to 6.8.7 cover six generic groups of such benefits. It is not intended that this is an exhaustive list.

6.8.1 Group productivity tools

New or enhanced processes or practices supported by group productivity tools refer to increasing the efficiency of all or a part of the organisation. Most automate systems[1] will fall into this category. The basis of the estimation of the benefits to be derived from this type of application is that of cost displacement or cost avoidance.[2] This usually involves comparing savings, which are often related to the reduction in the number of staff required or a reduction of the scale of asset holding required, to the cost of the acquisition and the operation of the technology. The benefit modelling required here is well known to accountants and is frequently practised in organisations. The type of analysis required to estimate these benefits is usually performed on a departmental or divisional basis. See Figure 9.3 (page 123) for an example of the calculation of this type of benefit.

Typical applications delivering this type of benefit are accounting systems, work flow systems, inventory and production management systems, to mention only a few.

---

[1] Automate systems are aimed at reducing the labour required for the manual aspects of clerical work.

---

[2] Cost displacement, or cost avoidance considers the cost of an investment and compares this to the other costs that the system has saved.

6.8.2 Individual or personal productivity tools

New or enhanced processes or practices supported by individual or personal productivity tools impact on the quantity and quality of the work of individuals. Sometimes this impact is sufficient to allow one person to do the work of several people, and in such cases the calculation of the benefit is relatively straightforward and requires the same type of benefit modelling as described for group productivity tools. See Figure 9.4 (page 124) for an example of the calculation of this type of benefit.

A problem arises here if, or when, the benefits are attributed to improvements in quality of work. In such cases an intangible benefit is under consideration and management judgement will need to be applied to arrive at an estimate of its magnitude for business case accounting purposes. This type of benefit modelling often requires benefit values to be negotiated by the principal stakeholders.

Typical applications delivering this type of benefit are spreadsheets, word processing, graphics packages, etc.

6.8.3 Informate the organisation

New or enhanced processes or practices supported by informate systems[3] (Zuboff 1988), refers to benefits associated with superior decision making and thus better performance due to individuals having more complete information about the circumstances of the organisation at their disposal. An information–decision making model may be constructed which will facilitate benefit modelling in this incidence (see Figure 9.6, page 126).

This model shows how information provided at the correct place, at the correct time and of the correct quality may lead to decisions. If these decisions are made appropriately and effectively they will produce actions and if executed efficiently and effectively will produce results. This is only the first step in benefit modelling which

---

[3] Informate systems are intended to provide management with extensive reports which will facilitate more effective management and control of the organisation.

describes how the informate process works. When this has been agreed the primary stakeholders will then have to reduce the outcome of the improved information to financial figures and produce a statement similar to the one shown in Figure 9.7 (page 127). As stated above this is not a trivial task and the preparation of these figures requires an understanding of how the information system will be used and how this use will impact on the requirement for resources in the organisation. Typically more demanding benefit modelling needs to be undertaken for these types of benefits.

Typical applications delivering this type of benefit are decision support systems and executive information systems.

6.8.4   Reduce time and space in business processes

New or enhanced processes or practices supported by IT that reduce time and space in business activities can lead to extensive benefits, many of which can be quantified in the same way as referred to above. In this case releasing office and/or factory space can directly reduce costs. Furthermore, sales can increase by more time being made available. Research conducted by Stalk and Hout (1990) show dramatic improvements in performance of organisations that improve their time cycles.

Typical applications delivering this type of benefit are workflow systems, e-mail and Internet communication based systems as well as scheduling systems, etc.

6.8.5   Create a corporate memory

New or enhanced processes or practices supported by creating a corporate memory[4] means that individuals are empowered to perform tasks requiring greater skills than they would otherwise be able to undertake. This can open up opportunities for more revenue, or it may allow costs to be contained. In either case the benefit modelling approach will not be dissimilar to that described above.

---

[4] Corporate memory is the ability of an organisation to recall useful information about the entities or processes required when conducting its business.

There are at least two basic types of applications that can deliver this type of benefit. These are database systems and include such applications as reservations and other type of order-taking systems. In addition to this there are an increasing number of expert systems or rule processing based applications which extend the corporate memory. Of course intranets are also an important part of the technology to support this type of benefit delivery.

6.8.6   Bind the organisation closely with clients and suppliers

New or enhanced processes or practices aimed at binding the organisation closely with clients and suppliers can be achieved through the use of inter-organisational systems such as EDI. These systems have a wide range of benefits that include the reduction of costs as well as increased opportunities for more revenue making activities. Relatively straightforward business modelling will be sufficient to forecast these benefits.

Typical applications delivering this type of benefit are POS or scanning systems in retail outlets. ATMs at banks are another example of such an application.

6.8.7   Introduce discontinuities by business process improvement

New or enhanced processes or practices, leading to the introduction of discontinuities[5], can be achieved through the application of business process improvement ideas (Hammer and Champy 1993). Once again this type of activity may either reduce costs or increase opportunities for more revenue making activities, or in fact both of these. Also opportunities to reshape or re-scope the business may be considered under this heading. Relatively straightforward business modelling will be sufficient to forecast these benefits.

There are many examples of applications delivering this type of benefit from most parts of a business. This would include any attempt

---

[5] The term discontinuity is used to describe a radical new approach to handle business activities. A classic example of this is abolishing documents such as invoices or receipts or cheques and working by lodging money directly into bank accounts.

to develop new or enhanced processes that are supported by IT investment.

6.9   The question of strategic alignment

Having established the corporate strategy that the organisation is following or attempting to follow, and having developed a list of applications and benefits which the organisation expects to obtain from the IT investment the next step is to establish if these are in alignment. An IT investment may be said to be in alignment with the corporate strategy if the processes or practices supported by the investment will directly assist or contribute to the organisation in achieving its strategy.

For organisations using the generic strategy model of cost leadership the question is then: '*Will the IT investment help reduce the direct cost and thus allow the organisation to get its price down or help it keep its low price position?*' For organisations using Porter's generic strategy model of differentiation the question is then: '*Will the IT investment help the organisation become or sustain itself as a provider of a high quality and price premium based product or service?*'

For organisations using value package strategy model the questions are similarly aimed at the three strategic alternatives.

6.9.1   Strategic alignment using the Porter model

A useful way of working with strategies and applications is to create a Function/Process-Strategy Table as shown in Figure 6.7. By listing the functions or processes that will be affected by the IT investment, and by establishing the strategic impact of each application within the IT investment, it is possible to arrive at a view concerning strategic alignment.

6.9.2   Strategic alignment using the three value package strategy model of Treacy and Wiersema

The four-column table in Figure 6.8 is useful if the three value package strategy model is being used.

6.9 The question of strategic alignment

Function/Process	Low Cost	Differentiation
Product design and development	Product engineering systems Project control systems CAD	R&D databases Professional multi-media workstations E-mail CAD Custom engineering systems Integrated systems to manufacturing
Operations	Process engineering systems Process control systems Labour control systems Inventory management systems CAM Systems to suppliers	CAM for flexibility Quality assurance systems Systems to suppliers Quality monitoring systems for Procurement systems suppliers
Marketing	Streamlined distribution systems Centralised control systems Econometric modelling systems Telemarketing	Sophisticated marketing systems Internet marketing Market databases IT display and promotion Web enhanced systems Competition analysis Modelling High service level distribution systems
Sales	Sales control systems Advertising monitoring systems Systems to consolidate sales function Strict incentive monitoring system	Differential pricing Office to field communications Sales support Dealer support Systems to customers
Administration	Cost control systems Quantitative planning and budgeting systems Office automation for staff reduction	Office automation for integration of functions Environmental scanning and non-quantitative planning systems

Figure 6.7 The Function/Process-Strategy Table – a list of applications to support the two generic strategies

Function/Process	Best product	Best total cost	Best total solution
Product design and development	CAD and CAM	Integrated systems to manufacturing Web marketing systems	R&D databases Professional multi-media workstations Email Custom engineering systems
Operations	Process engineering systems Process control systems CAD and CAM Systems to suppliers	Labour control systems Inventory management systems Procurement systems	CAM for flexibility Quality assurance systems Systems to suppliers Quality monitoring systems for suppliers
Marketing	Streamlined distribution systems Centralised control systems Econometric modelling systems	Sophisticated marketing systems Internet marketing Market databases IT display and promotion Web enhanced systems Telemarketing	High service level distribution systems Competition analysis Modelling
Sales	Sales control systems Advertising monitoring systems Systems to consolidate sales function	Differential pricing Office to field communications Sales support Dealer support Strict incentive monitoring system	Systems to customers
Administration	Cost control systems Quantitative planning and budgeting systems	Office automation for integration of functions Office automation for staff reduction	Environmental scanning and non-quantitative planning systems

Figure 6.8: The function/process-strategy table – A list of applications to support the three value package strategies

6.10 Practical examples

Considering the question of the strategic alignment, the example described in section 4.2.2 relating to the question of credit control shows clearly that this is a cost reduction activity. Thus this application would be best suited to support a low cost strategy as described by Porter or a best total cost and operational excellence strategy of Treacy and Wiersema.

With regards the second example described in section 4.3 relating to the question of sales administration, this application would be best suited to support the best total systems and customer intimacy strategy of Treacy and Wiersema shown in Figure 6.8. This sales administration application could also be seen to have low cost strategy implications as described by Porter and shown in Figure 6.2.

6.11 From benefit identification to benefit quantification

Having identified the applications that will allow benefits to be generated, the next step in the process is to attempt to quantify these benefits in terms of financial amounts. As was discussed in Chapter 4 some benefits are more easily quantified than others. Looking again at the IT benefit matrix in Figure 6.9, those benefits that relate to the top left quadrant such as staff reduction, lower assets, more sales, are relatively easy to quantify as is shown in Figure 6.10.

		Measurability High	Low
Tangible	High	Staff reduction Lower assets More sales	Better information
	Low	Faster information Positive staff reaction	Market reaction Access to new staff

Figure 6.9 IT benefit matrix

On the other hand the types of benefits described in the other three quadrants of Figure 6.9 require assumptions to be made concern-

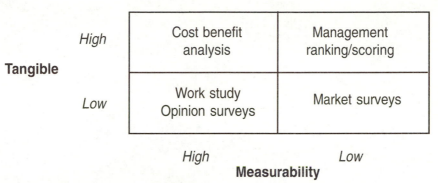

Figure 6.10 Benefit measurement techniques

ing the impact of the proposed benefit on the operation of the business. This is done by performing a detailed examination of the business process or practice which will be affected by the IT investment and then predicting the effect that this will have on the organisation's cost structure or income stream.

Where there is a degree of uncertainty as to the magnitude or the timing of the benefit then a risk or stochastic approach to this analysis may be performed as described in section 9.13.

6.12 Summary

Every organisation has a strategy. The corporate strategy does not have to be written down or stated explicitly.

New processes and practices supported by IT investment need to support the corporate strategy, i.e. be in alignment with it rather then work against it. If the IT investment and corporate strategy are not in alignment then there should be serious concern about the wisdom of the investment and consideration should be given to not proceeding with it.

Using a Function/process–strategy Table such as those shown in Figures 6.7 and 6.8 may be helpful in deciding if there is an appropriate alignment.

Forms to help produce the deliverables required from this phase of the business case are provided in Appendix A.

7 Technology issues

Despite years of technological improvements and investment there is not yet any evidence that information technology is improving productivity or other measures of business performance on a large scale - or, more importantly, significantly enhancing US economic performance. ..... the fundamental blame falls with organisations. Information technology holds great potential, but companies have failed to provide structures and processes that facilitate the use of information technology in ways that create significant net value.

(Loveman 1991)

It is very often impossible to ascertain immediately a project ends whether or not it has produced any or all of its expected benefits.

(Bradley 1996)

7.1   Introduction

No matter how good the proposed organisational process or practice intervention is from a business perspective, it is necessary to take a careful look at the technology issues which underpin the proposal to see if the IT project is actually viable. This is done in the technology report which also provides much of the detail required for the actual management of the tasks and the deliverables of the IT project. This part of the IT investment business case focuses on the projects' technobility,[1] doability and achievability.

The technology issues report gives the stakeholders a high level view of the key technological challenges influencing the IT investment business case. This complements the other aspects of the IT business case discussed earlier.

---

[1] Apoligies to readers for creating yet another piece of jargon and another hybrid word. Technobility refers to whether the proposed IT investment is technologically feasible or whether it is simply a pie in the sky hopeful expectation which cannot yet be achieved with the current state of our technology.

The impact of the technological investment is on the business processes themselves. However the technology itself also makes demands on the firm or organisation. These demands require a number of questions to be answered such as whether the technology will be in-house or bought-in. It will also be necessary to decide which technology to purchase (IT infrastructure, computers, communications and software).

The chosen technology directly influences the IT project management, including the timing of the delivery of the new processes or practices and the schedule for the establishment of the new procedures to realise the benefits of the investment.

7.2 Understanding required by the principal stakeholders

To evaluate the technological investment the stakeholders need to have a clear understanding of four key aspects of the IT investment being proposed. These are:

1 What is the proposed technology and what are what are the technological building blocks that have to be delivered to realise that solution?

2 How is the technical team who are to deliver the proposed processes organised?

3 What is the proposed schedule for the delivery of the solution?

4 What are the technology related costs of the project?

7.3 Create a technology statement

The first step in reviewing the technology involved in the IT investment business case is to create a technology statement. This is a high level summary of the technological solution and should address the following issues:

1 IT infrastructure

2 Hardware

3 Software

4 People

5 Budgets

6 Timing of the project.

7.3.1 IT infrastructure

The IT infrastructure section of the technology statement needs to outline the various IT platforms which the project will require. This involves looking at the organisation's IT architecture in order to establish what type of technological solution would comply with the organisation's long-term vision of how it wishes to employ IT.

Under the IT infrastructure section the question of outsourcing should be addressed. It is possible that the organisation may not regard the proposed IT investment as core to its activities and if this is the case, then outsourcing the project could well be the most sensible strategy. In addition, if there is any question that the organisation does not have the complete range of skills to complete all the technical work required for the success of the project, then any shortfall could be made up by engaging appropriate outsourcers.

7.3.2 Hardware

The hardware section of the technology statement is a list of the hardware required by the project. This needs to include the details of the processors, storage devices, monitors, printers and any other equipment. This hardware requirement may be set out in tabular format suggested by Figure 7.1 below.

Description	Function	Number	Size/Capacity	Special characteristics

Figure 7.1: The hardware requirement

This table summarises what hardware needs to be supplied in high-level non-technical terms. The special characteristics column is an important one that needs to be used to bring to the notice of stakeholders', unusual or high specification items.

The main issues that needs to be considered here are:

1 Reliability: if it is envisaged that the hardware needs to run for 24 hours/day then this could be noted here.

2 Special features: workstations needs to be portable and robust as they are going to be used in rough territory.

3 Speed: the server needs to be very fast, as it will be handling very large volumes.

7.3.3 Software

The software requirements details section of the technology statement is a list of the software required by the project. It can be presented in tabular format, much like the hardware requirements. This is shown in Figure 7.2.

Description	Build or Buy	Vendor	Support arrangements	Special characteristics

Figure 7.2: The software requirement

This table can be used to summarise the software items that are needed to build the system and commission it. Again the special characteristics column has an important role as it can be used to highlight software items that are important or unusual in some way.

An important consideration to be addressed under this section is that wherever possible the software should be purchased rather than be developed in-house. However, it is often the case that the software products offered for sale by vendors will not completely meet the organisation's requirements, and in such cases it will be necessary to either change the requirement or modify the software. Software modification can be as expensive as developing it *ab initio* and also exposes the system to a greater possibility of error.

7.3.4 People

People are required to realise the technological solution and implement the change process to put in place the proposed IT investment.

The presentation of the business case needs to show clearly how the staffing and expertise to deliver the solution can be assembled. This resource and expertise can come from within the organisation or be bought in in the form of consultants or contractors, etc. Once again a table can be used to present the information, as shown in Figure 7.3.

Job category	Number of staff	Expertise available strengths/vulnerability	Proposed start date	Proposed end date

Figure 7.3: People required to realise the solution

The table summarises the expertise available in-house in the IT function and other departments in the business for this project. It summarises the expertise at a high level and gives a feel of the size and depth of the support available for the technological solution. The information presented needs to cover both the development and operational expertise necessary to build, deliver, commission and maintain the technological solution. It will also highlight areas of particular strength and vulnerability. The Project Leader and his or her deputy should be named in this summary.

7.3.5 Budgets

An estimate of the capital expenditure for the IT investment is required. This can be divided into several different groups, including purchased outright, leased or rented, developed in-house, etc. Figure 7.4 is an example of the types of issues that need to be included here.

Item	Purchased outright	Leased or rented	Outsourced	Developed in-house
Purchases/Development				
Hardware				
Infrastructure				
Software (application)				
Software (systems)				
Software (comms)				
Commissioning				
Hardware				
Infrastructure				
Software				
Business system				

Figure 7.4: Budget for the technology required for the IT investment

7.3.6 Timing of the project

An important consideration is the lapsed time of the project and this issue needs to be addressed in the technology statement.

In order to be able to be confident about the lapsed time for the development of the IT project it is necessary to develop a high level project plan. This needs the work to be broken down into detailed activities and requires these to be programmed or scheduled in an appropriate manner. This aspect of the technology statement can be supported by the use of tools such as bar charts or critical path analysis techniques.

The schedules and timings around the building, delivery and commissioning of the technological solution are of key importance to the IT business case and its evaluation. There is practically always a serious time constraint on the realisation of a business plan once the decision to go ahead has been made.

To realise the technological solution, set up the required organisation and commission the whole business solution, a full project planning and control system will have to be elaborated and put in place by the project management. However, what is needed for the stakeholders to evaluate the business case and monitor progress is a high level summary of the schedule and subsequently variances from the plan.

7.4   Checklist to assist completing the technology statement

The following eight questions represent a useful checklist in producing the technology statement.

1   Is the proposed project technically doable?

2   Does the proposed technology conform to the organisation's IT architecture?

3   Should all or part of the project be outsourced?

4   Does the organisation have the IT competencies to deliver?

5   Can the IT team produce the required deliverables in an appropriate time scale?

6   Does the project budget look reasonable?

7   Is the organisation capable of absorbing the implications of the proposed system?

8   Is there any other compelling reason why the project should not be undertaken?

7.5   Summary

The technology issues are an important aspect of an IT investment business case. This dimension of the business case should be prepared primarily by IT professionals, in conjunction with the users/ owners.

If there is any question that the organisation is unable to provide adequate expertise to produce the technology statement then this may be outsourced to independent consultants. It is important not to outsource the development of this statement to prospective vendors of hardware, software and other IT services.

8 Risk – project and systems

The only fence against the world is a thorough knowledge of it.
John Locke, *Some Thoughts Concerning Education* (1693)

Risky investments may indeed carry a 'premium' reward but the existence of a precise relationship between the two cannot be demonstrated or verified as there is no objective and generally accepted method of evaluating risk.
Boyadjian and Warren (1987)

8.1 Introduction

Acquiring an understanding of the risks involved in an IT project is a central part of developing a comprehensive IT investment business case. The risk profile of the proposed IT investment needs to be clearly stated and if it is too high the IT business case should not be approved.

Risk appraisal in IT business cases has been frequently ignored and as a result many otherwise apparently sound IT business cases have actually been seriously flawed. When this happens IT projects fail.

Risk is always present in IT investments and this was well illustrated by Fortune and Peter when they described the London Ambulance Service computer disaster as follows:

The computer press is littered with examples of information technology fiasco or near disasters. An example is the computer aided dispatch system introduced into the London Ambulance Service in 1992. The £1.5 million system was bought into full use at 07:00 hours on 26 October and almost immediately began to 'lose' ambulances. During that and the next day less than 20% of ambulances reached their destinations within 15 minutes of being summoned, a very poor performance when compared with the 65% arriving within 15 minutes the previous May and the target set by the Government of 95%. The service reverted to semi-computerised methods during the afternoon of 27 October and then right back to manual methods on 4 November when the system locked up altogether and could not be re-booted. (Fortune and Peter 1995)

Although it is not essential that a full risk analysis be performed in order to produce an IT business case, a review of the more important risk issues should be addressed and incorporated into the IT investment business case.

8.2 Defining risk

Risk is a challenging concept to define, understand and ultimately to manage. This is primarily because the idea of risk can mean different things to different people. In terms of a formal definition, risk is described as

The probability that the actual input variables and the outcome results may vary from those originally estimated. (Remenyi 1999, Remenyi *et al.* 1993, Correia 1989)

This implies that the extent of the possible/probable difference between the actual and expected values reflects the magnitude of the risk.

Another way of looking at the definition of risk is provided by Chapman and Ward who state that:

A broad definition of project risk is 'the implication of the existence of significant uncertainty about the level of project performance achievable'. (Chapman and Ward 1997)

It should also be remembered that IT project risk management is a relatively new subject. According to Fairley:

Risk management in technical projects is a relatively new discipline, dating from around 1980... Risk management for software projects has been formalised within the past two years. (Fairley 1990)

He goes on to demonstrate the importance of understanding the importance of IT risk management by saying that:

Failure to do an adequate job of risk management leaves the outcome of a software project to a matter of luck and unfounded optimism. Systematic

risk management provides the framework, viewpoint and techniques needed to replace luck with engineering discipline. (Fairley 1990)

Clearly IT investment and the risks associated with it, should not be left to luck.

8.3 A 3 x 3 risk framework for IT project risk

The management of project risk can be a highly intuitive art (Turner 1995). However, there are some frameworks and guidelines to help assess and manage IT investment project risks. One of these frameworks is the nine variable approach proposed by Remenyi (1999) and described here in Figure 8.1.

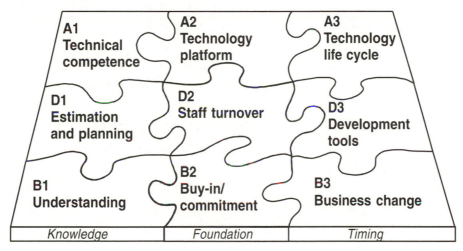

Figure 8.1:Key risks jigsaw

In this framework the risks are considered in terms of three major groups or categories. These are business risks, development risks and architecture risks. For each of these categories three individual risks are discussed. However in practice these risks may not balance out numerically in this way. On occasions there may only be one or two business risks, perhaps five or six development risks and only one or two technological risks, while on other occasions there may be seven or eight business risks and few development and architecture risks.

8.3.1 Risks categories: business, development and architecture

In Figure 8.1 the three major risk categories are represented by a jigsaw metaphor. The jigsaw is appropriate because it suggests the interlocking nature of these issues both horizontally within a risk category and vertically across domains or perspectives. Single IT development risks seldom occur. Thus it is important when thinking about IT development risks not to isolate or over exaggerate any one risk, as the components of one category of risk will invariably affect another category.

Although there may be any number of risks within a particular category, the three most important ones are discussed here. Obviously there are frequently more than three risks facing an IT project under each of these general areas. However it has been decided to focus on the three most serious potential problems that can be encountered. Of course what is considered to be a potentially serious problem is a function of an organisation's culture and its historic experience, but the three risks mentioned here would be considered to be serious in all organisations (Willcocks and Griffiths 1994).

The order of the risks within the jigsaw in Figure 8.1 is important. The most basic risks, which can easily destroy a project, and which it is quite possible for an organisation to be completely unaware of, are the business risks. Thus these are the most dangerous or difficult challenges facing an IT development project.

Development risks are usually considered the second most problematic, but they tend not to be as devastating to the project as the business risks.

Although still important, architecture risks are increasingly less threatening. This is not to say that an IT project cannot be wrecked by poor architecture decisions, but the technology at the turn of the century is more stable and reliable than ever before, and thus it is generally less problematical.

8.4 Other types of project risk

It is interesting to consider an alternative framework and in this case to look at how McFarlan (1990) views some the risks associated with information systems. He suggests that there are two main categories of risk, which are described as risks associated with failures of execution and risks caused by failures of conceptualisation. McFarlan's views are expressed as a matrix in Figure 8.2.

8.4.1 Risk associated with failures of execution

The risk associated with failures of execution can be categorised under three headings. These are the risks related to the structuredness of a project, the degree to which a project incorporates company-specific technology, and the size of the project. It is possible to use a 2 x 2 matrix to position the different levels of risk relative to the dimensions of structuredness of the project and novelty of the technology.

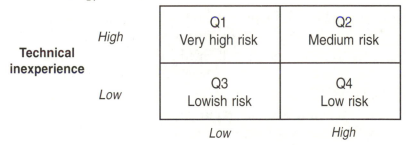

Figure 8.2: Matrix showing different degrees of risk (Source: McFarlan 1990)

The issue of the size of the project simply asserts that the larger the project the higher the risk, which in general terms is relatively obvious. There can however be exceptions to this proposition.

It is useful to consider each of the four quadrants in Figure 8.2 separately.

8.4.2 Quadrant 1 (Q1) – very high risk

In Quadrant 1 the project has low structuredness and makes extensive use of technology that is new to the organisation. Projects in this category should be considered by the organisation to be extremely high-risk projects.

According to McFarlan, project managers with both technical and people skills are required to make these projects work. PERT charts infer the projects' direction, but are otherwise not especially useful in establishing the time position for this class of project. McFarlan asserts that these projects are "not done until they are done!" Managers of these projects would expect numerous and frequent midstream changes. Such projects are always very expensive and their expense is derived primarily from the changes that are inevitably made to the original specification.

8.4.3 Quadrant 2 (Q2) – medium risk

In Quadrant 2 the project has both a high degree of structuredness and the use of technology that is new to the organisation. Projects such as these are generally medium risk projects. It is usual to expect mid-term corrections during these projects. PERT charts offer a fair representation of project status, but should not be totally believed as implications of the new technology that were not originally understood by the organisation may upset production plans. It is suggested that managers who are highly technically competent steer projects of this type.

8.4.4 Quadrant 3 (Q3) – lowish risk

In Quadrant 3 the project has a low degree of structuredness but uses technology that is known to the organisation. These projects are relatively lowish risk, but with potential hidden problems. Many projects in this category fail when they should succeed due to the lack of structuredness. To ensure success in projects such as these it is important that a strong and highly assertive user manager be placed in control or at the very least, high user involvement be sought.

This should be not only at the outset of the project, but on a continuous basis for the purpose of verification.

According to McFarlan the problem of risk with this class of project is the potential mid-stream change requests. Strict parameters need to be constructed around the project otherwise a continuous stream of change-requests from users will arise and the project will in all likelihood flounder and fail. The PERT chart offers managers a succinct view for these projects, but should be only utilised if a strong project manager can in some way incorporate a degree of structuredness.

8.4.5   Quadrant 4 (Q4) – low risk

In Quadrant 4 the project has highly specified outputs but low use of technology that is new to the organisation. These projects are low risk projects due to the tight definition of expected outputs and the use of familiar technology. As a result of the low risk level, companies can assign new and relatively inexperienced project mangers to these projects.

According to McFarlan, the use of PERT charts provides accurate indications of the completeness of the work. Due to the constricted nature of the outputs there is minimal user involvement necessary after the project commences. The low risk profile of these projects means that they should be successful with little need for risk management.

From the above it is clear that different types of projects have different types of implementation risk and, that different projects need different project management approaches if they are to be successful. These different types project management approaches should become apparent in the IT investment business case as a result of the assessment of the risk profile carried out at that stage.

The project management approach should flow from the project and not the other way around. Figure 8.3 indicates the management approaches that should be applied to different IT investment projects depending on the different risk profiles.

	Intensive risk management procedures	Strong focus on acquiring expertise
	Emphasise understanding the user	Routine management control

Technical inexperience — High / Low

Low — High
Structuredness

Figure 8.3: Management approaches to projects with different risk profiles

Figure 8.4 indicates the level of management activity that is required for different IT investment projects depending on the risk profile involved.

	Continuous management and costing intervention	Buy in skills and redevelop own staff
	Extensive user education	Low frequency low cost management

Technical inexperience — High / Low

Low — High
Structuredness

Figure 8.4: Management activity required with different risk profiles

8.5 IT systems risk

IT systems risk refers to failures of conceptualisation. This simply means poor ideas that were not likely to succeed from the beginning. McFarlan (1994) identifies the following categories of projects that are likely to fail due to poor conceptualisation.

1 A project that fails to meet customer requirements, no matter how technically sophisticated it is, is destined to fail. Technology can perform wonders, but if there is no market for the product or service supplied by the system, the project will fail.

2 The intended system may require behaviour that is not ingrained in existing users, such as the use of terminals or smart cards. As people shy away from change, such a system will fail. Thus if the project's ideas are rejected by the customer's culture then it will fail.

3 Systems incapable of evolving will fail. Evolution is an essential aspect of survival in the dynamic business environment of the modern commercial world.

4 The system not only fails to meet its stated performance objectives but actually disrupts the ability of the organisation to deliver its products or services.

5 Technology can be a double-edged sword, lowering entry barriers by reducing the costs of competing. Some Internet and WWW type applications may fall into this category of system.

6 Projects that are undertaken before all the tactical and strategic resources and commitments are in place are likely to fail.

The McFarlan approach described here is useful as a framework for thinking about risk and information systems, but it does not lead directly to an approach for the management of information systems risks. For more on this see the Butterworth-Heinemann book *Stop IT Project Failure*.

8.6 Incorporating risk in the business case

In producing the IT investment business case it is necessary to review the potential risks in term of the two categories described above.

Some IT investments will be more prone to implementation risks than conceptualisation risks, whereas others will have the opposite propensities. It is important that the principal stakeholders debate these issues thoroughly and that consensus is reached on what the major risks are, and how they might be minimised.

At this stage in the development of the IT investment business case a decision needs to be made as to whether or not the risk profile is acceptable. If it is then there is clearly no problem. If on the other hand the risk profile is too high then it is necessary to decide if a risk management programme might be able to sufficiently reduce the risk to allow the IT investment to proceed. If this cannot be done then the IT investment needs to be rejected. On the other hand if a risk management programme is agreed then this needs to be incorporated into the IT project manager's agenda when and if the proposed IT investment is approved and the project begins.

As mentioned above, risk management is an often neglected aspect of IT project management, and lack of attention to these issues has frequently resulted in IT project failure.

8.7   Summary

An assessment of the risks of the project and of the system is an integral part of the IT investment business case, as it is essential that the principal stakeholders have an appreciation of the potential problems that the proposal might face.

It is important to address the issue of risk under two main categories. The first relates to the risks associated with the implementation process that might cause the project to fail. The second relates to the risk of the system failing to deliver the type of improvements to the business processes and practices that had originally been envisaged.

By reviewing all these issues and incorporating them in the IT investment business case it is possible to manage the project in such a way that the risk of failure will be significantly reduced.

IT investment business cases should not be approved unless the risk issue has been addressed and the stakeholders agreed that the project risk profile is acceptable.

9 | Business case accounting

Long run is a misleading guide to current affairs. In the long run we are all dead.
(Keynes 1923)

There are three kinds of lies: lies, damned lies and statistics.
Benjamin Disraeli (quoted in Neider, 1959)

9.1 Introduction

Having decided the direction of the firm's IT investment at a business level through the development of a macro model and a meso model, it is then necessary to perform some detailed analysis of the financial impact the proposed investment is likely to have on the organisation. This has been referred to as the micro model in Chapter 4 and usually implies the conducting of a detailed financial study that involves business case accounting or cost-benefit analysis.

9.2 Basic approach

The techniques used for this type of analysis include capital investment appraisal, which involve the calculation of financial ratios such as the payback, the return on investment (ROI), the net present value (NPV) and the internal rate of return (IRR).[1]

It is normal practice not to just produce one financial statement or micro model but rather to produce several different scenarios or financial pictures. However sometimes there is only one IT investment being offered and if this is the case then it is advantageous to produce a financial statement showing what the situation would look like if no action is taken and the status quo is maintained.

---

[1] See Appendix B for definitions and explanations of the range of investment performance statistic generally used in business.

In addition to this what-if [2] analysis showing what will happen if some of the assumptions are not realised should accompany the micro model.

9.3 Concepts required for business case accounting

There are many different financial concepts and issues involved in business case accounting. It is essential that all these elements be addressed in the financial analysis. Unlike IT benefits, the concept of IT costs is well understood and therefore does not need elaborate definition. However, there are a number of different financial issues that need to be considered when preparing an IT business case. These include:

◆ Hidden costs
◆ Opportunity costs
◆ Marginal costs
◆ Time value of money
◆ Discounted cash flow
◆ Interest rate or Hurdle rate or cost of capital
◆ Horizon or economic life
◆ Terminal value.

9.3.1 Hidden costs

A hidden cost is a not so obvious cost of IT that may in fact appear in another department or function, but as a result of computerisation. According to Willcocks (1991) operations and maintenance costs are sometimes considered to be hidden and these can amount to as much as 2.5 times the development and installation costs over the first four years of the life of an IT project. As the impact of IT has become better understood there is much more understanding of IT costs, and thus less scope for costs to be hidden.

---

[2] What-if analysis is sometimes referred to as sensitivity analysis. Although from a modelling point of view this is not strictly correct, both what-if analysis and sensitivity analysis do serve a similar function in the sense that they indicate how the outcomes will change under different assumptions.

9.3.2 Opportunity costs

The opportunity cost of an investment or project is the amount the firm could earn if the sum invested was used in another way. Thus the opportunity cost of a computer system might be the amount that could be earned if the funds were invested in the core business, or if the funds were placed in an appropriate bank account.

9.3.3 Marginal costs

Cost-benefit analysis is traditionally performed on a marginal cost and revenue basis. This means that numbers are based on the variable cost associated with the new IT investment and that this excludes the general overhead. When it come to benefits evaluation the same rule applies and thus only new or extra benefits should be included. This marginal costing approach prevents double counting of either the cost or the improvements.

9.3.4 Time value of money

The concept of the time value of money refers to the fact that money today is worth more to the organisation than money tomorrow. It is on the notion of the time value of money that discounted cash flow is based, which is one of the most important methods for the evaluation of any investment proposal.

9.3.5 Discounted cash flow

Discounted cash flow is the way that the concept of the time value of money is operationalised. Cash flow is discounted by calculating its present value, which requires the sum to be reduced by a rate of interest equivalent to the organisation's investment opportunity rate. This discounting is done for each year that it takes to obtain or to make the payment.

9.3.6 Interest rate or hurdle rate or cost of capital

The interest rate or hurdle rate or cost of capital are three different terms for the rate of interest that is used in the discounted cash flow calculation. Whatever name is used for this interest rate, the number used needs to represent the rate which the organisation can earn on the funds under its control. Thus this is also sometimes referred to as the required rate of return.

9.3.7 Horizon or Economic life

The Horizon or Economic life of the investment is the period for which it is believed that the investment will be effective and thus for which it will earn an economic return. This is one of the most difficult issues to estimate for an IT investment.

9.3.8 Terminal value

The terminal value of an investment is the amount for which the investment could be sold at the end of its economic life. In this respect IT investment frequently has little or no terminal value.

9.4 Detailed cost items

The following is a fairly comprehensive list of the major costs that an information system might incur:

◆ Direct costs of hardware and software purchased, hired or leased;

◆ Costs of communications media, notably telephones and digital lines.

◆ Cost of Internet and Web connections;

◆ Support and maintenance costs, either due to in-house specialists or third-party vendors;

◆ Consumables such as hard disks, diskettes, CD-Roms, printer ribbons, toner cartridges, etc;

◆ Ancillaries accessories such as new furniture for computer workstations, acoustic hoods for printers, uninterruptable power supplies, cabling;

◆ Bureau charges for access to hardware and software;

◆ Costs incurred by IS planning, management, development, analysis, programming;

◆ IS specialist staff costs, including recruitment and training as well as salaries;

◆ Consultant, analyst and contractor costs from third party firms;

◆ Training and tutoring costs incurred by non-IS staff when learning to use the new system;

◆ Time spent by non-IS staff and management for developing, introducing and evaluating the system;

◆ Time spent by non-IS staff and management in sorting out problems on the new system;

◆ Modifications to the site, buildings and offices necessary to accommodate the new system;

◆ Transition costs when converting to the new system, for activities such as rewriting software, setting up files and databases, converting existing data, parallel operation of new and old systems, use of temporary staff during the transitional phase, etc;

◆ Suppliers' charges for installation and delivery of system components;

◆ One-off staff payments to encourage transition to the new system, or redundancy payments if applicable;

◆ Insurance charges for loss or damage to the equipment and consequential loss of income if the equipment is out of service for a significant period;

◆ Charges for provision of backup equipment or services, to cater for the possibility of system failure;

◆ Documentation costs for initial development and for ongoing updates at regular intervals;

◆ Costs involved in upgrading software and hardware;

◆ Business continuity guarantee or disaster recover costs;

◆ Costs due to having a system with a limited growth capacity, or due to having a non-standard system requiring special attention;

◆ Costs due to inefficient operation, such as poor cash flow, lack of accurate information for planning and decision making;

◆ Costs due to delays in system implementation, thereby losing the benefits that may have possibly been gained in that period;

◆ The cost of failure if the system proves ineffective, or is constantly out of action due to hardware or software problems.

The above list includes both hard and soft costs. Hard costs are those which are readily agreed by everyone as being attributable to the IS and which are easily captured by the firm's accounting system. Among hard costs are payments to vendors for hardware and software and IS staff salaries as well as the costs for site modification, consultants, etc.

Soft costs are those costs that cannot be readily agreed as being directly attributable to the IS effort and which are not easily identifiable in the firm's accounting records. Soft costs include items such as users' time in learning systems, users' time in sorting out problems, reduced productivity encountered during the learning experience of a new system by operators, etc.

9.5   Pattern of costs

It is interesting to note that the distribution of costs when implementing new IT systems has changed dramatically over the past 20 years. It is generally understood that the organisational costs have increased from about 20% to 50%. Of course this trend will continue for quite some time. This is clearly shown in Figure 9.1.

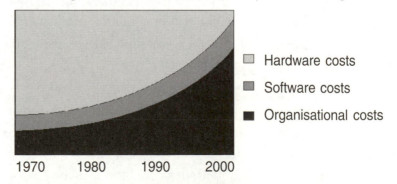

□ Hardware costs

■ Software costs

■ Organisational costs

1970   1980   1990   2000

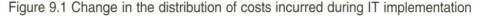

Figure 9.1 Change in the distribution of costs incurred during IT implementation

The change in the proportion of cost is due not only to the decline in hardware cost but also to the absolute rise in organisational cost. Organisational costs have escalated dramatically because of the much more comprehensive types of systems that are now being implemented by organisations. The more comprehensive the IT investment the more organisational expense which will be required.

The figures included in the cost estimates of a system should be based on the ownership costs over a projected five-year system life. Systems lasting longer than this period will in some senses produce a bonus for the organisation. Systems that do not remain in place for five years could produce negative results, but this does not mean that the investment should not be undertaken.

9.6   Sources of cost estimates

Obtaining reliable cost estimates has always been difficult and this has contributed to the on-going problems with IT project budgets.

There are various sources of cost estimates. These include obtaining quotations from the different contributors to the project. These could include suppliers, contractors, consultants, outsourcers, etc. The cost of these resources can often be negotiated on a fixed fee basis which may then be reliably used in the business case accounting exercise.

Other sources of costs are estimations of the development work required of the system's in-house team. This will include an analysis of the problem, the creation of a project specification and the amount of time required to develop or write code for the system. There are also the in-house costs of training the staff. The commissioning cost may also be incurred internally. This type of cost estimation is subject to considerable error and some organisations cope with this by comparing the proposed project with previous similar developments. This is, of course, a form of internal benchmarking and can draw on corporate best practice if this has been recorded. Many of the organisational costs shown in Figure 9.1 fall into this category and these are not easy to estimate.

The idea of benchmarking can then be taken outside the organisation where estimations of costs can be gathered by looking at similar projects.

Whichever approach is taken towards cost, estimates have to be produced with considerable care as they are always prone to error. A provision for contingency for cost escalation is often used as a way of coping with this. Another approach to the uncertainty of costs is the use of risk or stochastic analysis, which will be discussed in section 9.13.

9.7 Sources of benefit estimates

As already mentioned in both Chapter 4 and Chapter 6 it is quite challenging to produce detailed financial estimates of the anticipated benefits. However some attempt needs to be made in this respect. The key to producing competent financial estimates is to understand how the business process and practices which will be affected by the IT investment will actually change the way costs are incurred or revenue is generated or assets are used. If this is achieved, then useable figures may be estimated. In situations where there is a material amount of uncertainty as to the likely result of the IT investment, a stochastic approach as described below should be used.

9.8 Different approaches to business case accounting

Cost-benefit analysis can be defined as the process of comparing the various costs of acquiring and implementing an information system with the benefits the organisation derives from the use of the system. In general, cost-benefit analysis should be performed on a marginal-costing basis. This means that only additional costs incurred by the new system should be included. Likewise only marginal benefits, i.e. new or additional benefits, should be compared to the costs.

It is sometimes suggested that only benefits are difficult to estimate. However, as many IT projects over-run their cost estimates, this is clearly not the case. Considerable care must be given to cost estimation, especially where software development is concerned. Also, on-going costs should be carefully scrutinised.

Different approaches to cost-benefit analysis are required for auto-mate, informate and transformate investments. The following are among the most important.

9.8.1   Cost displacement

Cost displacement considers the cost of the investment and compares this to the other costs the system has saved. This is typically used in the more traditional data processing environments where computers are used to replace clerical workers or even sometimes blue-collar workers. Cost displacement is not really appropriate for situations where the IT system is intended to add value, rather than reduce costs. A cost displacement justification is a classic automate or efficiency situation, although it may also have informate implications. Figure 9.2 shows an example of cost displacement analysis of an investment for one year. It should be noted that the costs and benefits are marginal ones and therefore will not necessarily display the relationship described in Figure 9.1.

This cost displacement approach to assessing an IT investment proposition is an ex-ante analysis of what the firm hopes to achieve. It is nothing more than a statement of intent. To ensure that these intentions are carried out, a list of details about the system and the environment in which it will function must also be supplied. It is sometimes preferable to perform this type of analysis over a number of years and Figures 9.3 and 9.4 show the cost displacement approach for three and five years. There is considerable debate as to whether IT investments should be planned on a three, five or even seven-year horizon. Some firms use a three-year period for personal computers, a five-year period for mid-range systems and a six or seven-year period for mainframes. However, a growing number of practitioners believe that three to five years is the maximum period for which IT should be planned. This, however, does produce problems for some large-scale systems that can take three years to develop. Obviously in such cases a longer time horizon would need to be used.

9.8 Different approaches to business case accounting

Using IT to automate jobs, 1 year		All costs in 000s
Cost displacement	*Year 0*	*Year 1*
Set up costs		
Hardware including PCs, LANs and other peripherals	125	
Software including spreadsheet, WP, database and comms.	98	
Training	75	
Installation and testing	52	
Total	350	
Monthly on-going costs		
Staffing, including support		28
Maintenance and upgrades		20
General		8
Total		56
Monthly benefits		
Reduction in clerical salaries		42
Reduction in supervisory salaries		8
Reduction in other staff costs		13
Office space released		5
Other office expenses saved		3
Total		71
Improvement per month		15
Annual net benefit		180
Annual ROI		51 %
Simple payback		2 Years

Figure 9.2: The cost displacement approach – 1 year

Using IT to automate jobs, 3 years		All costs in 000s		
Cost displacement	*Year 0*	*Year 1*	*Year 2*	*Year 3*
Set up costs		1	2	3
Hardware including PCs, LANs and other peripherals	125			
Software including spreadsheet, WP, database and comms.	98			
Training	75			
Installation and testing	52			
Total initial cost	350			
Monthly On-Going Costs				
Staffing, including support		28	29	31
Maintenance and upgrades		20	21	22
General		8	8	9
Total costs		56	58	62
Monthly Benefits				
Reduction in clerical salaries		42	44	46
Reduction in supervisory salaries		8	8	9
Reduction in other staff costs		13	14	14
Office space released		5	5	6
Other office expenses saved		3	3	3
Total benefits		71	74	78
Improvement per month		15	16	17
Annual net benefit	-350	180	189	198
Simple annual ROI		51%	54%	57%
Simple payback		2 Years		
Cost of capital	20%			
Discounted annual net benefit	-350	150	131	115
Discounted payback		3 Years		
Net present value		46		
Internal rate of return		28%		
Profitability index		1.13		

Figure 9.3: The cost displacement approach – 3 years

Using IT to automate jobs, 5 Years		All costs in 000s				
Cost displacement	*Year 0*	*Year 1*	*Year 2*	*Year 3*	*Year 4*	*Year 5*
Set up costs						
Hardware including PCs, LANs and other peripherals	125					
Software including spreadsheet, WP, database and comms.	98					
Training	75					
Installation and testing	52					
Total initial costs	350					
Monthly on-going costs						
Staffing, including support		28	29	31	32	34
Maintenance and upgrades		20	21	22	23	24
General		8	8	9	9	10
Total costs		56	58	62	64	68
Monthly Benefits						
Reduction in clerical salaries		42	44	46	49	51
Reduction in supervisory salaries		8	8	9	9	10
Reduction in other staff costs		13	14	14	15	16
Office space released		5	5	6	6	6
Other office expenses saved		3	3	3	3	4
Total benefits		71	74	78	82	87
Net improvement per month		15	16	17	17	18
Annual net benefit	-350	180	189	198	208	219
Simple annual ROI		51%	54%	57%	60%	63%
Simple payback		2 Years				
Cost of capital	20%					
Discounted annual net benefit	-350	150	131	115	100	88
Discounted payback		3 Years				
Net present value		234				
Internal rate of return		47%				
Profitability index		1.67				

Figure 9.4: Cost Displacement over five years

9.8.2   Cost avoidance

A cost avoidance analysis is similar to cost displacement, except that no cost has been removed from the system because the introduction of the IS has prevented cost from being incurred. Cost avoidance, like cost displacement, is typically used in the more traditional data processing environments which address automation and efficiency

Using IT to automate jobs, 5 Years		All costs in 000s				
Cost avoidance	Year 0	Year 1	Year 2	Year 3	Year 4	Year 5
Set up costs						
Hardware	345					
Software	299					
Training	345					
Installation and testing	179					
Total	1168					
Monthly on-going costs						
Staffing, including support		55	58	61	64	67
Maintenance and upgrades		78	82	86	90	95
General		44	46	49	51	53
Total		177	186	196	205	215
Monthly benefits						
Staff not required		120	126	132	139	146
Other costs avoided		85	89	94	98	103
Total		205	215	226	237	249
Improvement per month		28	29	31	32	34
Annual net benefit		336	353	370	389	408
Annual ROI		29%	30%	32%	33%	35%
Simple payback		3 Years				
Cost of capital	20%					
Discounted annual net benefit	-1168	280	245	214	188	164
Net present value		-484				
Internal rate of return		-2%				
Profitability index		0.59				

Figure 9.5: The cost avoidance approach

and is therefore sometimes thought to be generally less relevant to more modern IT applications. However, a cost avoidance analysis may also be used to support an IT business case for infrastructure investment. Figure 9.5 shows an example of cost avoidance analysis for an investment over five years.

9.8.3   Decision analysis

Decision analysis attempts to evaluate the benefits that can be derived from better information, which is assumed to lead to better decisions. In turn, better decisions are believed to lead to better performance. As it is hard to define good information, let alone good decisions, cost-benefit analysis performed using this method is difficult.

Decision analysis is a classic informate situation and requires a financial value to be associated with information. In some cases, it is relatively easy to measure the effect of information, although there will frequently be considerable noise in the environment that can obscure the effects of the system. The key to decision analysis is to perform rigorous business analysis of the situation before the introduction of the proposed technology. The types of business relationships at work and their effects on each other must be understood. Also how the proposed IS will disrupt these business relationships, hopefully in a positive way, needs to be explained. A model of how information is used in the firm to make decisions and how these decisions impact upon actions which in turn affect performance is useful when conducting decision analysis. Such a model is shown in Figure 9.6.

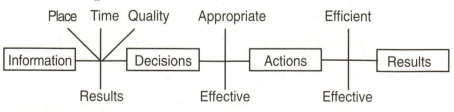

Figure 9.6 Decision analysis model

Figure 9.7 shows an example of decision analysis. This case relies on understanding how the firm's credit control works, how the cash flow functions, and how investment availability impacts sales.

Using IT to improve performance through more information, 5 Years				All costs in 000s			
Decision analysis	Year 0	Year 1	Year 2	Year 3	Year 4	Year 5	
Set up costs							
Hardware	555						
Software	450						
Initial training	250						
Commissioning	150						
Installation and testing	300						
Total	1705						
Monthly on-going costs							
Staffing, including support		292	307	322	338	355	
On-going training		50	53	55	58	61	
Maintenance and upgrades		95	100	105	110	115	
General		120	126	132	139	146	
Total		557	586	614	645	677	
Monthly benefits							
Reduction in bad debts		25	25	25	25	25	
Interest earned by faster receipts		50	53	55	58	61	
Reduction in obsolete Inventories		120	126	132	139	146	
Increased sales due to better availability		430	452	474	498	523	
Total		625	656	686	720	755	
Improvement per Month		68	70	72	75	77	
Annual net benefit	-1705	816	842	869	897	927	
Annual ROI		48%	49%	51%	53%	54%	
Simple payback		2	Years				
Cost of capital	20%						
Discounted annual net benefit		680	585	503	433	373	
Net present value		2573					
Internal rate of return		41%					
Profitability index		2					

Figure 9.7 An example of decision analysis

Using IT to improve salesperson's productivity Investment costs for 10 systems	All costs in 000s	
Set up costs		
PCs, cellular modems and peripherals	125	
Database, spreadsheet, WP and communications	23	
Training	30	
Installation and testing	60	
Total initial costs	238	
Monthly on-going costs		
Staffing, including support		10
Communications costs		2
Maintenance		5
General		3
Amortisation		6
Total monthly costs		26
Monthly benefit analysis		
Average no. of sales calls per day		6
Average value of sales per call		1.70
Reduction in average sales call time from 35 to 15 minutes		20
Reduction in time required for daily form filling from 60 to 10 minutes		50
Total Time Release — (50+ (6x20))		170
Average travel time between sales calls		25
Average number of additional sales calls resulting from IT investment 3		
Monthly revenue analysis		
Resulting additional revenue		5.10
Profit margin %		4.00%
Daily profit improvement from 10 systems		0.20
Monthly profit improvement per salesperson (22 days per month)		4.49
Monthly profit improvement from 10 systems		44.88
Annual profit improvement		539
Annual operating cost of system		312
Annual net benefit		227
ROI		95%
Payback		1 Year

Figure 9.8 An example of impact analysis

9.8.4 Impact or time release analysis

Impact analysis attempts to quantify the effect IT can have on the physical performance of employees. Impact analysis may have elements of automate, informate and even transformate, depending on the exact circumstances involved.

The primary benefit of time release is that staff can do other work, and when this leads to acquiring extra sales it can contribute to transforming the business. Figure 9.8 shows an example of impact analysis.

9.8.5 Transformate analysis

The type of analysis used to assess a transformate opportunity is the same as that employed for any strategic investment. Strategic investments often involve many considerations that are particularly difficult to quantify. Issues such as competitive advantage, market share and new product development are just a few examples. Strategic investments are frequently considered so important that a full ex-ante cost justification cannot be undertaken, or if it is, the results of the analysis are simply ignored. Statements such as 'it's too important to ignore' or 'the cost of not doing it will be crippling' are frequently heard in association with strategic investments. Therefore, strategic investment appraisal studies will often contain more words than numbers. The descriptive part of the proposal will contain words such as those shown in Figure 9.9.

---

1 This investment represents an extremely attractive opportunity for the firm to penetrate a new and profitable market

2 The demand in the new market is likely to increase at a compound rate of 25% pa for the rest of the decade.

3 The new production facility will reduce our costs so substantially that we will be able to undercut both our nearest competitors.

4 Client service will improve substantially.

Figure 9.9: Strategic considerations

Good practice, however, requires some numeric analysis to be performed. As transformate or strategic investments will have a longer time implication than efficiency or effectiveness investments, the simple ROI and payback methods are not adequate. The time value of money based techniques such as discounted cash flow need to be used.

9.9 Combining these approaches to business case accounting

From time to time an IT investment will affect the business processes and practices in several different ways. For example the same investment will have a cost displacement effect as well as a transformation effect. When this occurs the different approaches described above will be combined in the one micro model.

9.10 Difficulty in estimating investment variables

Traditional cost-benefit analysis is undertaken using discounted cash flow techniques involving estimates of the investment amount, the annual benefits and the cost of capital. All these variables are difficult to estimate. However, the cost of the firm's capital is frequently considered the most difficult variable to determine. The rate of interest the firm pays on its debt, or an arbitrarily chosen hurdle or discount rate is sometimes used as a surrogate for the cost of capital.

9.10.1 Deterministic versus stochastic

IT systems evaluation can be undertaken in several different ways using a variety of measures and at least two different processes. The two processes discussed here are the *deterministic* approach using single point estimates for the input values and generating a single estimate for the result, and the *stochastic* approach which uses ranges as input and generates a range of results. The stochastic method is sometimes referred to as *simulation* or *risk analysis*.

Deterministic analysis assumes a certain world where the exact value of input variables can be known. Once the values of these inputs are entered a unique result, determined by the logic of the algorithm and the precise data, is calculated. Because ex-ante investment analysis exclusively uses estimates of future values for the investment amount in the form of the on-going costs and the benefits, it is frequently said that as soon as the single point values are determined, the input and output will be wrong.

Risk analysis, on the other hand, attempts to accommodate the inherent variability in the input estimates and produces a result that more closely reflects the level of uncertainty frequently experienced in the real world.

In situations where uncertainty is small, deterministic models can provide suitable solutions. However, it is more likely that uncertainty in the input variables, evidenced by their variability, is likely to relatively high and therefore this uncertainty will have to be taken into consideration.

This uncertainty can be captured by specifying a probability distribution for each of the input variables – such as investment, cash flows, and cost of capital. There are many candidate probability distributions that can be usefully employed for this purpose. Some of the more useful distributions are likely to be the uniform, the triangular and the beta.

Operationalisation of the above uses the Monte Carlo[3] method. This involves generating a range of outcomes for the input variables, e.g. investment, described by some specified probability distribution, and then evaluating the behaviour of an associated output variable, e.g. internal rate of return. The Monte Carlo method can also be used to establish how robust and sensitive the outcomes are with respect to the assumptions concerning the input variable(s).

For more on the properties of a number of probability distributions, and guidance on how to generate random samples from these distributions, see Johnson and Kotz (1970) and Gonin and Money (1990). Also within all major spreadsheets there is a facility to create these types of distributions.

---

[3] This approach is referred to as the Monte Carlo because it relies on the production of random values within the ranges specified for the variables and is therefore likened to the chance aspect of a roulette table.

9.11 Using deterministic analysis

Figure 9.10 is the input form of a deterministic model for capital investment appraisal in a spreadsheet. All the data are single point estimates.

Capital investment appraisal system							
A deterministic model							
		Cash-out	Cash-in				
IT investment - cash out		350,000	-350000				
Net IT benefits	Year 1		66106				
	Year 2		99902				
	Year 3		120901				
	Year 4		194590				
	Year 5		249671				
Fixed cost of capital or interest rate		25%					
			Y1	Y2	Y3	Y4	Y5
Forecast inflation rates			2%	3%	3%	4%	4%

Figure 9.10: Input form for a deterministic model

The use of inflation adjusted cash flow techniques requires that all figures used actually represent cash dispensed or received by the firm. Therefore, profit figures that include non-cash items such as depreciation or reserves should not be included. Figure 9.11 is an investment report based on the input in Figure 9.10, which shows a number of different investment measures including payback, NPV, PI, IRR, etc.

An important feature of this spreadsheet model is the use of variable costs of capital or interest rates. These interest rates may be used to reflect either anticipated rates of inflation, or more generally, to account for an increasing risk profile. The further into the future the estimated benefit the greater the degree of uncertainty or risk, and therefore the higher the discount or interest rate associated with the investment. The high interest rate has the effect of reducing the future value of the benefit.

Investment reports on IT system				
Payback in years and months	3	years	4	months
Rate of return(%)	41.78%			
NPV at fixed discount rate (FDR)	-9760			
Profitability index at FDR (PI)	0.97			
Internal rate of return (IRR)	23.91%			
Variable discount rates (VDR)				
NPV at VDR	-55414			
Profitability index (PI) at VDR	0.84			
Discounted payback at FDR in years and months	5	years	1	month

Figure 9.11 Results produced by the deterministic model

The results in Figure 9.11 are, of course, highly dependent upon the assumptions made concerning the cost of capital, the investment amount and the annual cash flows. As these future estimates are always uncertain it is appropriate to perform what-if analysis on these assumptions. The table in Figure 9.12 indicates the way in which the NPV and the PI are related to the cost of capital.

Sensitivity analysis on varying fixed cost of capital				
	NPV	PI		
	-9760	0.97		
20%	38609	1.11		
21%	28150	1.08		
22%	18102	1.05		
23%	8448	1.02		
24%	-834	1.00		
25%	-9760	0.97		
26%	-18349	0.95		
27%	-26615	0.92		
28%	-34575	0.90		
29%	-42242	0.88		
30%	-49631	0.86		

Figure 9.12 Effect of cost of capital on the NPV and PI

Figure 9.13 shows the combined effect of differing investment amounts and different costs of capital on the project. Looking at this table it can be seen that with an investment of £320,000 and a cost of capital of 21% the resulting NPV will be £32,598.

Sensitivity analysis on NPV with varying investment and fixed cost of capital						
-9760	20%	21%	22%	23%	24%	25%
300000	88609	78150	68102	58448	49166	40240
310000	78609	68150	58102	48448	39166	30240
320000	68609	58150	48102	38448	29166	20240
330000	58609	48150	38102	28448	19166	10240
340000	48609	38150	28102	18448	9166	240
350000	38609	28150	18102	8448	-834	-9760
360000	28609	18150	8102	-1552	-10834	-19760
370000	18609	8150	-1898	-11552	-20834	-29760
380000	8609	-1850	-11898	-21552	-30834	-39760
390000	-1391	-11850	-21898	-31552	-40834	-49760
400000	-11391	-21850	-31898	-41552	-50834	-59760
410000	21391	-31850	-41898	-51552	-60834	-69760
420000	-31391	-41850	-51898	-61552	-70834	-79760

Figure 9.13: Effect of variation in cost of capital and investment amount on NPV

9.12 Using risk analysis

As mentioned previously, the risk of an investment is the potential of input/output variables to fluctuate from their original estimates. As in the vast majority of cases input/output variables do fluctuate, risk analysis accommodates this by allowing ranges, rather than single point estimates, to be entered into the model. It is generally easier to confidently state that an investment will be between 200,000 and 300,000[4] than it will be 250,000.

There are a variety of techniques available to assist management in assessing the extent and the size of the risk inherent in a particular

[4] In the context of this chapter it has been assumed that the distribution of the variable specified by this sort of range is uniform i.e. there is equal probability of the outcome being any value between the minimum and the maximum.

investment. For the purposes of this chapter the size of the risk involved may be regard as the range of the estimates.[5] There are at least three generic approaches to identifying and assessing risk:

◆ Group brainstorming
◆ Expert judgement
◆ Assumption analysis.

9.12.1 Group brainstorming

Group brainstorming uses group interaction to identify the variables that carry the most exposure to variability. Once the variables have been identified, the group then attempts to quantify the limits of the variability as well as the probability associated with the range of possible inputs and outputs. Brainstorming groups may meet several times before the estimates of the variables are finalised.

9.12.2 Expert judgement

Expert judgement uses experienced individuals who are aware of the factors causing the investment potential to vary. This is the quickest and easiest way of identifying risk, but considerable care must be taken when choosing the expert.

9.12.3 Assumption analysis

Assumption analysis requires the detailed questioning of each assumption. This analysis requires each assumption to be modified in such a way that circumstances will be evaluated which are disadvantageous to the investment. The effects of the changes in assumptions are then used as part of the range of variable specification.

9.13 A risk analysis example

Figure 9.14 shows the agreed-upon minimum and maximum investment data for the capital investment model used earlier in this chapter.

---

[5] There are other ways of accommodating risk in capital investment modelling such as increasing the cost of capital when projects are perceived to be exposed to a higher than usual risk.

9.13 A risk analysis example

The initial investment will be between £350,000 and £400,000. Similarly the IT benefits for years 1 to 5 are also specified as ranges, for example in year 1 the maximum benefit is estimated at £70,000 and the minimum value of the benefit is stated at £60,000. Similarly, the cost of capital is not known, but it is estimated at between 20% and 30% per annum.

Input form for risk analysis													
		Minimum	Maximum										
IT Investment - cash out		350000	400000										
Net IT benefits	Year 1	60000	70000										
	Year 2	95000	105000										
	Year 3	120000	130000										
	Year 4	180000	200000										
	Year 5	200000	250000										
Fixed cost of capital		20.00%	30.00%										
Inflation adjusted	Y1 Min	Y1 Max		Y2 Min	Y2 Max	Y3 Min	Y3 Max	Y4 Min	Y4 Max	Y5 Min	Y5 Max		
cost of capital	20%	25%		30%	35%	35%	40%	40%	45%	45%	50%		
Mark variable to report with	X		NPV (FDR)										
an X in the appropriate box			IRR										
			NPV (VDR)										
	N.B. You must mark ONLY ONE box with an upper case X												

Figure 9.14 Risk analysis input form

9.13.1 The results of risk analysis

From the input data in Figure 9.14 a range of summary statistics can be produced and Figure 9.15 shows the effect of applying the risk analysis to the NPV calculation, and Figure 9.16 show the results graphically.

The results shown in Figures 9.15 and 9.16 would be regarded as being of relatively high risk. The reason for this is that the most likely outcome is an NPV of -43,218 with a standard deviation of 28,800.

Summary statistics for	NPV (FDR)		Frequency Table	
				NPV (FDR)
Mean	-43218.641		-113610.068	1
Standard deviation	28800.542		-98938.691	27
Range	146713.778		-84267.313	125
Minimum	-113610.068		-69595.935	247
Maximum	33103.709		-54924.557	328
No. of recalculations	2000		-40253.179	366
			-25581.802	349
			-10910.424	251
			3760.954	185
			18432.332	104
			33103.709	17

Figure 9.15 Results screen for risk analysis on NPV

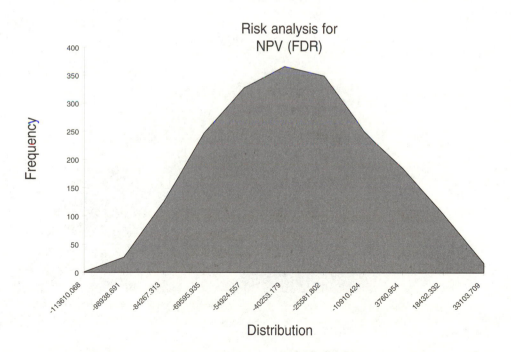

Figure 9.16 Graphical representation of risk analysis results for NPV at a FDR

9.13 A risk analysis example

Summary statistics for	IRR		Frequency Table	
				IRR
Mean	0.203		0.163	1
Standard deviation	0.016		0.171	12
Range	0.083		0.179	105
Minimum	0.163		0.188	249
Maximum	0.246		0.196	341
No. of recalculations	2000		0.204	335
			0.212	325
			0.221	306
			0.229	208
			0.237	104
			0.246	14

Figure 9.17 Results screen for risk analysis on IRR

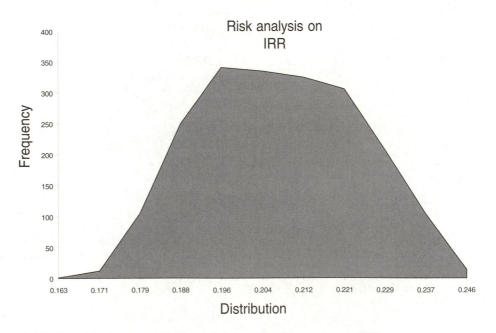

Figure 9.18 Graphical representation of risk analysis results on IRR

In Figures 9.17 and 9.18 the risk analysis has been performed using a different set of input data, and looks at the effect of the ranges of data on the IRR.

These results can be regarded as a relatively low risk. The most likely outcome of this investment is an IRR of 20%.

This kind of spreadsheet-based risk analysis provides a convenient way to adjust the input data in order to re-evaluate the risk patterns. Viewing the results graphically assists in the interpretation of the risk factor.

9.14 Investment decision rules

Every organisation will have its own investment decision rules. Some organisations will not invest in IT unless a payback of two years or less is forecast. Other organisations are less concerned about payback and thus by implication, ROI.[6] Such organisations often focus on NPV and IRR.

In discounted cash flow analysis an investment is said to be acceptable if the NPV is equal to or greater than zero. However some organisations believe that for IT projects there should be a sizeable positive NPV which they regard as a safety factor. Organisations that have difficulty in deciding on the value of their cost of capital, use the IRR and they will often specify an arbitrary value, such as 25%, which if the project exceeds it, will be accepted. For more detail on these investment statistics see Appendix B.

9.15 Summary

There are a number of different approaches to business case accounting or cost-benefit analysis that range from single point estimate techniques to rather sophisticated risk or stochastic analysis. In developing an IT investment business case it is important to choose the appropriate level of sophistication and not to spend an excessive amount of time on the financial numbers.

[6] The ROI is by definition the reciprocal of the payback. See Appendix B.

In some cases, where the amounts are small, it may not be necessary to perform any business case accounting or cost-benefit analysis at all.

Business case accounting is only at best a part of the IT investment business case and as such needs to be seen as a supporting tool to the main justification of the IT investment proposal.

10 Evaluating a business case

The ideas of economists and political philosophers, both when they are right and when they are wrong, are more powerful than is commonly understood. Indeed the world is ruled by little else. Practical men, who believe themselves to be quite exempt from any intellectual influence, are usually the slaves of some defunct economist.

(Keynes 1936).

Customer-intimate companies know their customers don't buy a product or a service. They buy its benefits.

Wiersema (1996)

10.1 Introduction

As the twenty-first century approaches, investment in IT is of increasing importance to business and other organisations. This is for a number of reasons including the fact that information is playing a greater and greater role in many organisations. This has been well illustrated by Drucker when he said:

We will have to learn, before understanding any task, to first ask the question, 'What information do I need, and in what form, and when?' The next question people have to learn to ask is 'To whom do I own which information and when and where'. (Drucker 1997)

It is not a simple matter, however, to successfully implement IT investments. Peters refers to this when he says:

Information Technology is a major enabler. But there's lots, lots more to the story. (Peters 1992)

Consequently it is important to thoroughly understand the new processes and the business outcomes which will be supported by the proposed IT investment and this is best achieved by preparing a comprehensive IT business case.

10.2 The preparation of a business case is challenging

Investment in business has always been a difficult issue. The difficulty has been that the decision to invest is by nature based on a number of forecasts, which may or may not be reliable. The aphorism that 'prediction is always difficult, especially when it is about the future' clearly expresses the problem. As a result, the performance of some investments has been successfully predicted, while for others it has not. Sometimes it is just impossible to even guess what the future holds. Writing on the issue of the returns of future investments Keynes points out:

The affair was partly a lottery, though with the ultimate result largely governed by whether the abilities and character of the managers were above or below the average. Some would fail and some would succeed. But even after the event no one would know whether the average results in terms of the sums invested had exceeded, equalled or fallen short of the prevailing rate of interest; though, if we exclude the exploitation of natural resources and monopolies, it is probable that the actual average results of investments, even during periods of progress and prosperity, have disappointed the hopes that prompted them. Businessmen play a mixed game of skill and chance, the average results of which to the players are not known by those who take a hand. (Keynes 1936)

One of the most significant comments made by Keynes about the nature of the investment decision is related to our need to achieve and also to take a risk. Thus he states:

If human nature felt no temptation to take a chance, no satisfaction (profit apart) in constructing a factory, a railway, a mine or a farm, there might not be much investment merely as a result of cold calculation. (Keynes 1936)

However, fortunately it is generally recognised that business is different to the roulette table or the racecourse. The risk or chances which are taken in business need to be calculated risks, and the calculations need to be based on sound evidence about the nature of markets, organisations, technology and people's performances. Thus there is a need for a comprehensive business case when large sums of money are to be invested.

10.3 Investment in IT

This is especially true in the case of IT where the record of success has not been as great as many would have wished. During the 1980s and the 1990s a number of surveys were conducted which have shown that the return on IT was poor. According to the OECD (1988), IT is not linked to overall productivity increases. Romtech (1989) stated that 70% of users declared that their systems were not returning their company's investment. An Amdahl (1988) survey showed that only 31% of companies reported that the introduction of IT had been successful. According to Hochstrasser and Griffiths (1990) only 24% of firms claim an above-average return on capital from their IT and 20% of IT spend is wasted. Willcocks (1991) pointed out that 30–40% of IS projects realise no net benefit what-soever, however measured.

Perhaps the greatest insult of all to IT and information technologists came from the *Economist*. It proclaimed that manufacturers who purchased information technology in the late 1970s and the early 1980s earned such a low return on the money invested that they:

would have done better ... to have invested that same capital in almost any other part of their businesses. (*Economist* 24 Aug. 1991)

10.4 The need for an IT investment business case

As mentioned earlier in this book, the result of this criticism is that there is considerable concern about the wisdom of investment in IT and this has produced a need for carefully worked out business justifications for all such investments. In some organisations this has meant the production by accountants of detailed financial esti-mates of the costs and the changes in cash in-flows which may be produced as a result of investment in IT. However, this type of ap-proach has in turn been criticised for the extensive number of as-sumptions that are sometimes made and the way in which intangi-ble benefits are sometimes converted to monetary values.

10.5 The hallmark of a professionally produced business case

The primary hallmark of a professionally produced IT investment business case is that it represents a consensus of understanding and commitment on the part of the principal stakeholders to introduce new or enhanced business processes or practices. This consensus of understanding and commitment will have been arrived at through a process of research, evaluations, discussions and dialogues whereby differences and conflicts will have been resolved. This may have required several reiterations of the IT investment business case document before agreement has been reached.

These reiterations can take a number of weeks, or for large-scale IT investment even a number of months, and many draft documents will have to be produced before the final IT investment business case emerges. Furthermore this process can be expensive. However the return on the professionally produced IT investment business case can be substantial, as the process of producing this document can dramatically reduce an organisation's propensity to embark upon unsound IT investments. Unsound IT investments are enormously wasteful and thus extremely expensive and preventing this type of problem is financially, very beneficial.

The main features of the professionally produced IT investment business case are:

1 An agreement that the proposed IT investment will suitably enhance the organisation's business both in terms of the required return on investment and strategic and tactical considerations;

2 A comprehensive understanding of all the key issues involved, technological and others, in making an IT investment successful;

3 The full commitment of the principal stakeholders who will have to play a part in ensuring the success of the IT investment;

4 An understanding of the major risks involved with the investment;

5 A platform which may be used as a management tool for ensuring that the project is on track and thus that a suitable return is achieved on the investment in new or improved business processes and practices.

Finally, it is perhaps the fact that a professionally produced business case can also be used as a project management framework, which can ensure delivery of IT benefits that make it most powerful.

10.6 Summative and formative evaluation

The evaluation of an IT investment business case is essentially a summative process in which it is decided whether the proposed investment is good enough for the organisation to commit the funds, time and effort required. The result of this summative process will be either to proceed with the IT investment or to decline the opportunity i.e. a *yes* or *no* outcome. However it would be unusual if at the end of this process there was not some aspect, implicitly or explicitly, of a formative evaluation. This simply implies that at the end of the IT investment business case exercise there would be some learning for the organisation. This learning should take place irrespective of whether the IT business case is accepted or not.

This learning will afford the organisation the opportunity to improve its ability to produce more comprehensive IT investment business cases. In so doing this will help the organisation have a more thorough understanding of how it may enhance its business processes and practices and how it may do this with the support of IT investment.

In fact while the distinction between summative and formative or learning evaluation is an important one, they are very closely aligned and there will frequently be some aspect of both approaches present in any evaluation situation.

10.7 A checklist for evaluating a business case

The function of an IT investment business case is to present a convincing argument to management to spend a sizeable sum of money and a considerable amount of effort on an investment project to improve a process or practice. To do this successfully the IT business case needs to comprehensively address the five key areas that have formed the major part of the discussion in this book, and which are shown again in Figure 10.1.

10.7 A checklist for evaluating a business case

At the end of this exercise there will be five sections to a report and each of these have to be appraised both separately and as a whole. In order to assist in the appraisal of these sections of the IT investment business case the following checklist of questions may be helpful. Note that financial issues are closely linked to the business outcome, but specific financial questions need to be answered. Similarly operational issues are mainly to do with implementing the technology.

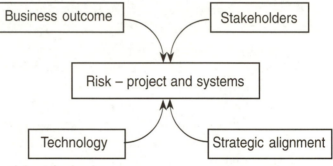

Figure 10.1: The five modules of a business case

Business outcome issues

Business outcome: Is the problem or opportunity well enough understood? Is there a clearly articulated macro-model, meso-model and micro-model? Is it clear that the proposed system directly support the organisation's vision, mission, strategy? Does the proposed IT investment make good business sense?

Business case accounting: Are sufficient funds available to finance the project? Is the estimated ROI or NPV adequate to cover the organisation's cost of capital? If this is not the case are there other strategic reasons for this investment that makes it necessary despite the poor forecasted financial return?

Stakeholder issues

Has a user/owner prepared the business case? Who is the sponsor, the champion and the project manger? Does the project have adversaries? Are all the important stakeholders committed to making this IT investment a success?

Strategic alignment

Is it clear that the proposed IT investment directly supports the organisation's strategy? If it does, then to what extent is it counter-productive or work against the strategy?

Technology issues

Technology issues: Does the organisation adequately understand the proposed technology? Is the proposed technology readily available? Is there adequate backup and business continuity provided?

Operational issues: Does the organisation have the right people in place and are the time scales proposed realistic? Has adequate attention been given to matters such are training and testing, etc? Has outsourcing been given appropriate attention?

Risk issues

What are the main risks? Can action be taken to manage and thus minimise this risk? Is the risk profile acceptable to the stakeholders?

10.7.1 Evaluation section by section

As mentioned above each of the five different sections of the report need to be reviewed separately. If any one of these five sections fails to satisfy the group of primary stakeholders then the viability of the whole IT investment project needs to be questioned. For example, even if the other dimensions of the IT investment business case are showing satisfactory indications, if any one of them is not up to the required standard, or has some major unanswered questions associated with it, the IT investment should not proceed.

10.7.2 Overall evaluation

The checklist shown above can be represented on a matrix that allows each of the five different sections of the report to be given a rating. The required rating, which is shown in the second column of Figure 10.2 and is called the Base Score, is the minimum score that is needed for each of the different sections of the report described in the IT investment business case checklist. A scale of 1 to 5 is used and the Base Scores are the target scores required. A score of 5 reflects an aspect of the IT investment business case which needs to show the highest compliance with the standards laid down by the organisation, while a score of 1 would correspond to an issue of relatively less importance and thus such an aspect of the IT investment that the business case need not live up to the theoretically required standard. In the third column each issue has been rated in terms of how ready for action it is thought to be. From Figure 10.2 it is clear that the level of business case accounting is not considered sufficient and on an overall basis the business case in its current state falls 5 points short of the total ideally demanded by the organisation.

Issues	Base Score	Score
Business outcome	5	4
Business case accounting	3	1
Stakeholders	4	3
Strategic alignment	4	4
Technology	3	4
Operational	4	3
Project risk[1]	–3	–2
Total	**20**	**17**

Figure 10.2: Matrix for assessing business case preparedness

If an IT investment business case were assessed as shown in Figure 10.2 it would be necessary to return to the business case process and revisit all the components except that relating to the strategic alignment as this has scored 4 out of 4 and technology, which is thought to exceed to stated requirements.

10.8 Weighting and scoring for prioritising projects

Where several projects are to be compared against each other then one approach that extends the above method is to establish prioritisation based on the above list of criteria using weights and scores. These criteria can be weighted and scored and be used to calculated a value which can then be compared for different IT investment opportunities.

[1] In this type of summary evaluation, risk is normally regarded as negative. Thus a higher risk score will reduce the attractiveness of the proposed IT investment.

This process could be routinised by preparing a spreadsheet that will calculate these prioritisation values based on the value that is the product of the weights multiplied by the scores. There are a number of ways of weighting these variables, but one is to establish a weighting system for each of the seven issues on a scale of, say, 1 to 5 where 5 reflects an issue of the highest importance to the organisation and 1 would correspond to an issue of relatively less importance. Note, all the weighting numbers are probably stated as positive numbers.

Having established the weights of the different variables the next step is to review, for the purposes of scoring, each of the different projects. Each project would be awarded a score on a scale of, say, 1 to 10. This score is a subjective evaluation of the IT investment agreed to by the group of principal stakeholders. If there is a difference of opinion among the various stakeholders then an average value may be calculated. If there is a large number of stakeholders involved then a standard deviation may also be calculated.

A value for each variable or issue is then calculated by multiplying the weight by the scale and the values for each project are then summed or totalled.

Care needs to be taken with the variable that represents the risk. Risk is generally regarded as a problem. If this is the case then the score allocated to the risk variable should be stated as a negative, which will mean that the risk value will be calculated as a negative and this number will reduce the total value for the project. If on the other hand the risk variable is seen as a positive opportunity to earn a greater return on the IT investment then the risk variable should be stated as a positive and this number will increase the total of the value for the project.

Using the type of weighting and scoring method described here the project with the highest value would then appear to deserve to have the highest priority. Of course this is a rather mechanistic view and there may well be special circumstances which dictate that a project with less that the top score be considered for top priority. Nonetheless this approach tends to give the project prioritisation decision some structure. Figure 10.3 is an example of how these seven issues could be rated and prioritised across three different projects.

Issue	Project 1			Project 2			Project 3		
(Wt = weight and Sc = score)	Wt.	Sc.	Value	Wt.	Sc.	Value	Wt.	Sc.	Value
Business outcome	5	4	20	5	10	50	5	7	35
Business case accounting	2	1	2	2	8	16	2	10	20
Stakeholders	5	3	15	5	4	20	5	3	15
Strategic alignment	5	4	20	5	6	30	5	7	35
Technology	2	4	8	2	5	10	2	9	18
Operational	3	9	27	3	7	21	3	8	24
Project risk	−4	10	−40	−4	3	−12	−4	9	−36
Total			52			135			111

Figure 10.3: Weighting and scoring method for prioritising projects

In Figure 10.3 Project 3 shows the highest value and therefore would appear to deserve maximum prioritisation.

10.9 Summary

An IT business case is essential to the professional management of information systems resources.

The production or development of an IT investment business case is a business process in its own right. Although the output of the IT investment business case is a document it is sometimes argued that the real value of this exercise is in the learning which takes place during its development process.

It is not trivial to produce a competent business case for an IS project. In fact to produce a credible one is not a simple matter and requires considerable time and resources. However the return on a professionally produced IT investment business case can be substantial, as the process of producing this document can dramatically reduce an organisation's propensity to embark upon unsound IT investments and thus the benefits of having a business case should far exceed the cost.

11 Using the business case for IT project management

There is nothing more difficult to take in hand, more perilous to conduct, or more uncertain in its success, than to take the lead in the introduction of a new order of things

Machiavelli, *The Prince*, (1532)

The Somebody Else's Problem field is much simpler and more effective (than other ways of making things invisible) ... This is because it relies on people's natural predisposition not to see anything they don't want to, weren't expecting, or can't explain.

Douglas Adams, *Life, the universe and everything*, (1982)

11.1 Introduction

Successful IT project management is not so much about acquiring and using project management tools such as critical path analysis or work breakdown approaches, as about achieving and sustaining a set of common understandings of what types of interventions are required to ensure that the target business processes and practices are enhanced by the supporting IT.

The IT investment business case may be used as part of a basis for IT project management. Using it in this way allows for a new approach to more successful IT project management. This chapter considers a framework for the implementation of this new approach to IT project management, through a suitable programme using the IT investment business case as the starting point and the principles of continuous participative evaluation as discussed in Chapter 3 (Sherwood-Smith 1989; Finne *et al.* 1995; Remenyi *et al.* 1997) as a method for tracking the progress of the IT project.

A key issue to better IT project management is the paying of appropriate and continuous attention to the real business objectives of the information system being developed. Once these business objectives and the implementation risks associated with them, have been clearly understood and agreed to by all the information system's primary stakeholders, it is necessary to continuously track the project's performance and the objectives and the risks, until the information system is delivered.

An important aspect of this new approach to IT project management is the notion of continuous assessment and co-evolution. Care needs to be taken to ensure that as the project progresses the stakeholders' understanding of the business objective grows. This requires that there should be a mutually sustained understanding of what the outcome of the information system will be and results in a process of continuous confirmation that the project is on track and that it will produce appropriate benefits. Professionally conducted IT project management can make a major contribution to the successful implementation and subsequent management of information systems, and especially to the eventual acceptability of the information system to all its stakeholders.

11.2 Phases to IT project management

There are three distinct phases in a successful IT project management programme.

The first of these may be referred to as *Setting the Course* which involves the development of the IT investment business case under the headings of business outcomes, stakeholders, strategic alignment, technology and risk.

The second phase is the *Formative Evaluation* and involves closely assessing the progress of the project, while phase three is called *Moving Forward* which provides a feedback loop which, by the way, should be available, not only during development, but also throughout the entire life of the project.

11.3 A reiterative process

Thus, this IT project management programme is a reiterative process whereby a system's requirements are refined or co-evolved in a controlled manner. Figure 11.1 shows the reiterative nature of this activity.

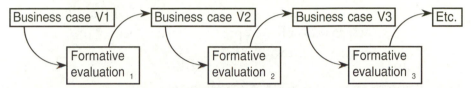

Figure 11.1: Reiterative process of formative evaluation

An IT project management programme needs to begin when the information system is first conceptualised and stay in place at least until the information systems is commissioned.

The application of this framework or method to IT project management leads to a non-traditional[1] approach to information systems conceptualisation and development as well as to the subsequent assessment of the effectiveness of the information system. In addition, through a high degree of openness, which involves expecting information systems professionals to play a co-evolutionary role together with line managers and users, as well as financial and administrative staff, more effective information systems may be developed. This means that IT need no longer be tied into single purpose-built developments created by technicians, but can be the product of collaboration.

Although it is not possible to be prescriptive about how an IT project management programme will or should be conducted on a day-to-day basis, it is possible to say that in general it consists of the three distinct phases described above as:

[1] Traditionally information systems were developed by information systems people, usually quite technical individuals, with only the minor involvement of line management or users/owners during the system's specification stage and perhaps during the system's testing. Accounting and financial staff were occasionally invited to help prepare an ex-ante or summative evaluation of the investment as part of a feasibility study.

1 Setting the course by developing the three initial pictures;

2 The formative evaluation process;

3 Moving forward towards the objectives after closing of the feedback loop.

These phases are shown in Figure 11.2. In addition the process by which these phases operate to ensure focused professional IT project management will be explained.

11.4 A route to successful IT implementation

The diagram in Figure 11.2 may be seen as a chart describing the route through which a successful information system's implementer needs to navigate or travel.

At the outset the principal stakeholders need to produce the comprehensive IT investment business case. This is not a trivial process and will require a considerable amount of time and the involvement of a number of different stakeholders. This ultimately leads to the authorisation of the project aimed at achieving these outcomes and the IT development work commences.

Project management techniques are then used to control the day-to-day work. However, this new IT project management programme means that all those involved are sensitive to how the project is progressing and to whether or not it is possible to make improvements to either how the information system is being developed or to the actual business solution itself.

Formative evaluation sessions are held at regular, planned intervals during which progress is reviewed. A key aspect of this review is the notion of continuous assessment and co-evolution as the stakeholders navigate towards an effective information system's solution to their business problem or opportunity. This means that as the IT project progresses the stakeholders' understanding of the business objectives and requirements grows, and thus there develops a mutually sustained understanding of what the outcome of the information system will be. This effectively requires that there is a process of continuous confirmation that the project is on track and that appropriate benefits will be realised. This also means that there is a continuous evaluation of the IT investment business case as it is possible for the requirements to change so much that the original IT investment business case to be no longer relevant.

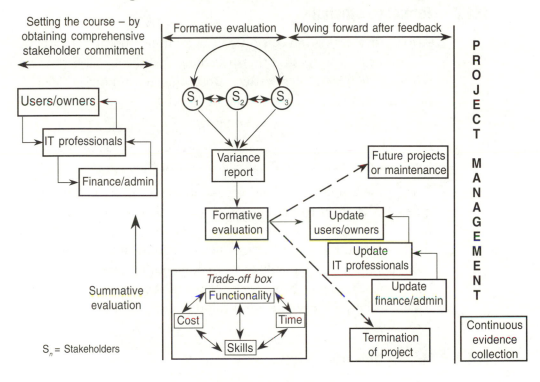

Figure 11.2: Phases of an IT development project

Figure 11.2 also shows how the three sets of stakeholders, who have already been described as users/owners, IT Professionals and finance and administration people, interact. Each of these stakeholder groups have their own interests in the IT project.

The three main phases shown in Figure 11.2 are the reiterative process whereby these three groups of stakeholders agree on an IT investment business case and that the IT investment business case is approved by a summative evaluation i.e. *Setting the course*; the *Formative evaluation* phase and the *Moving forward* phase.

11.4   A route to successful IT implementation

11.4.1   Setting the course

The processes required here have been extensively discussed in the earlier chapters of the book. Once the summative evaluation has approved the IT investment business case the project begins.

11.4.2   Formative evaluation

A formative evaluation session will determine whether or not the IT project is on track and that no changes to the specification are required or it may suggest that substantial rethinking is needed, perhaps even project abandonment.

As can be seen from Figure 11.2 all the major stakeholders need to be involved during the formative evaluation sessions as input or feedback may be required from all or any of them.

During the formative evaluation session there will frequently be requests for changes to the proposed system. Each suggested change needs to be assessed to ensure that it is important to the success of the IT project. Proposed changes always require either more funds, more people and their skill and of course more time. Often there has to be a trade-off between what would be ideally desired and what can be produced within available budgets, time and people resources.

11.4.3   Moving forward

Moving forward refers to accommodating changes and progressing the IT project. If the suggested changes are considered to be important then one of four possible courses of action need to be taken.

If the suggested change is relatively small then it is quite possible that it may be accommodated within the original scope of the IT project. If this is the case then the IT project plan is simply modified and work continues.

If the suggested change is substantial then the proposer of the change needs to find the funds necessary to have them undertaken. The proposer of the changes may also need to produce a case for the delays which may be inherent in the suggested changes. If this is so, then once the changes have been funded and the time delays agreed, the IT project plan is modified and work continues.

Sometimes there will be either insufficient additional funds or the project will be too urgent to be delayed in order to accommodate the proposed changes. In such cases the required changes are noted and it is agreed that they are to be incorporated into the systems when the second release is made available. Some organisations do not favour the notion of second releases and in such cases the required enhancements are often undertaken as maintenance.

The final alternative result of the formative evaluation is that the IT project is actually terminated. This can occur when a change is proposed which is so profound that it throws into question the wisdom of the IT investment itself. This seldom occurs. However it is generally believed that it should take place more than it does. IT projects tend not to be terminated but often run to the end only to find that the solutions which they represent are no longer relevant or required.

11.5 Summary

Incorporating the IT investment business case into a new approach to IT project management has a number of advantages to offer. This is required because IT project management does not have an especially good track record. There are frequently problems with budget over-runs as well as delays to promised delivery dates. Furthermore there is far too high an incidence of wasted resources where the delivered system is no longer relevant to the business. This new approach to IT project management helps alleviate all these problems.

But perhaps the single most important aspect of this new approach to IT project management is the fact that it builds consensus among the various stakeholders by recognising their co-creation and co-evolutionary status in developing business solutions. Not only will this approach produce more IT benefits, but it will also reduce waste.

11.5 Summary

It will tend to decrease the amount of time it takes to deliver effective systems which help produce direct business benefits and thus substantially improve the utilisation of the organisation's resources.

12 | A case study

Proton Electronics Limited

The establishment of a series of process benefits and their estimated financial value

Real problems are hard to spot, especially for managers so involved in day-to-day operations that they have inadequate perspective to see the big picture.
(Wiersema 1996, p49)

The case study presented in this chapter describes an organisation that is in need of a business case for its IT investment. Working through this case study will give the reader an opportunity of putting into practice the concepts discussed in the earlier chapters.

In order to illustrate the fact that many of the issues involved in preparing a business case need to be addressed and understood from the perspective of a number of different stakeholders, the case study is presented as a series of recollections from different members of the organisation's management.

Close examination of the details of the case study will reveal a wide range of business outcome issues, including costs and benefits, as well as the other dimensions of the business case, including stakeholders, strategy, technology and risk.

In thinking about the preparation of a business case for this IT investment, it needs to be remembered that there is no one correct way of presenting a business case and that the organisation's business culture is important in this respect.

Some suggestions as to how the business case for Proton Electronics could be presented are available from the Butterworth-Heinemann Web site at **http://www.bh.com/samples**.

Background to the company

The following is a briefing given by Mr George Edwards, Managing Director of Proton Electronics Ltd to Petra Jones as he engaged her as a new business systems development manager.

We have spent more than £7 million on the ISIS/2000 system in the past three years and I just don't know whether or not that money was well spent. Perhaps I should have kept the money in the bank or spent it on developing the business or just use it for dividend payments for the shareholders.

Of course the vendors at the time of signing the contract were full of promises about benefits. They talked about automate, informate and transformate benefits, but I haven't seen anything that I could personally present in a convincing manner to my colleagues on the board. It is true that some of the staff are very keen on the system but they just don't seem to be able to produce credible financial figures. ISIS/2000 is an integrated sales order entry, inventory management, credit control, production scheduling and transport scheduling system. It was acquired to replace a number of separate mainframe systems, some work which was previously done on stand alone personal computers and other manual systems. ISIS/2000 was 18 months late on being commissioned and cost nearly twice as much as the original estimate. Thus it got off to quite a poor start and its image especially among top management has never really recovered.

To add to this unsatisfactory situation there have been as many grumbles from staff about the new system as there were about the old one. In fact some members of staff are suggesting that we need to replace ISIS/2000 with ISIS/2020 which has already been estimated will cost nearly twice as much again.

But we will not spend another sou until we nail down exactly what we have had from this system and why we might need to change again.

We also need to have a better plan than we had before, but no one around here seems to know how to initiate or control that process.

The main objective of your job at present is to understand the circumstances surrounding ISIS/2000 and to come up with a detailed and accurate evaluation of what we have been doing over the past few years as well as some sound suggestions as to how we might proceed into the future.

In conversation with the Chief Accountant

An extract of a conversation with Thomas Williamson, the Chief Accountant of Proton Electronics Ltd.

I wasn't really consulted about the new system. The first I heard of it was when I was invited to a sales briefing which was given by Fred Johnston from ISIS Corporation. Fred Johnston is a very competent computer sales person but I am not all that sure that he puts Proton Electronics interests ahead of his desire to make another sale and improve his commission income! At the time I heard his presentation the decision was largely wrapped up. There wasn't that much need for me to get involved. You see, in Proton Electronics the accounting function is largely one of record keeping and therefore as Chief Accountant I do not really get involved with the decision making process.

And of course the financial director Gerry King has delegated the DP function entirely to me. Gerry will retire next spring and it is clear that he has no wish to be involved with computers. Thus as director or head of this firm's EDP I am fully responsible for the smooth running of that function.

This responsibility is entirely delegated by me to Joe Slithers who is our EDP manager. He has 25 or so people in his team as well as some contractors and other outsourced resources and he runs his show according to a strict budget which we set each year. As long as he keeps within his budget, he is doing a great job as far as I am concerned.

ISIS/2000 was, and I guess still is, an operational system with only minimal financial accounting implications so when I attended the sales presentation I felt that it was just as well that I was not too involved. I was pleased that at last something was being done about the credit control systems as we have traditionally experienced a reasonable bad debt situation, about 0.1% of turnover. Our industry has lots of small operators and when there is a down turn in the economy it is hard to know who will go to the wall next.

And I have some interest in the inventory levels which seem to be continually rising. The production people just keep focusing on economies of scale without the slightest care about locking up working capital. So when I heard that ISIS/2000 would release 5% to 10% of the working capital I was rather pleased that this critical issue was being addressed by the data processing people. We do not take a very rigorous approach to ascertaining our cost of capital but our general rule of thumb is that a suitable rate is in the order of 20% and our directors normally regard that rule of thumb estimate as sufficiently accurate for our purposes.

Of course there was also talk about ISIS/2000 being able to deliver better client service and about the possibility of releasing staff from the sales order processing offices. This is not really my concern. You had better talk to Kathy Newman the personnel officer and Frank O'Reilly the Sales Manager.

Yes, there were problems with its commissioning. I don't really know the details. The system was quite late being installed. It was something to do with the performance or the hardware or maybe it was the software. I am not really sure. Response times were slow and there were queues for printing, etc. I know much of the software had to be re-written and bigger and better and much more expensive processors had to be purchased. None of this went through Slithers' budget, of course. It was all treated by the Managing Director in terms of his executive powers.

The problems with ISIS/2000 did cause us to look at outsourcing the whole IS function and although we did have a number of outsourcing organisations in to talk to us about the advantages of going this way and we did indeed outsource some of our IS activities, we decided pro tem not to proceed further with this option for the time being. We realise how important this decision is and we need to move quite cautiously on issues which are of such strategic importance to the firm.

I can let you have a copy of last year's P & L and Balance Sheet. It is a summary of the main financial items.

In conversation with the Personnel Officer

An extract of a conversation with Kathy Newman, the Personnel Officer of Proton Electronics Ltd.

The question of staff savings were on the agenda right from the very beginning, at least from the beginning of my involvement. I was invited to advise on how we should handle relocation of staff and/or redundancy if necessary. These discussions took place about a month before the first system was installed.

It was suggested that the sales office could be run with four or five less people after the introduction of ISIS/2000. As there are five sales offices throughout the firm this meant that there would be a saving of 20 to 25

Profit and Loss Account for the year ending 31 December 199X

	(in £'000,000)
Revenue	345
Cost of sales	205
Gross Profit	140
Gross Profit %	40%
Overheads	
Administration	20
Cost of funding	20
Legal expenses	2
Marketing	11
Research and development	1
Salaries	17
Transport	5
Travel and entertainment	3
Total indirect expenses	79
Net Profit	61
Net Profit %	18%
Corporation tax	20
After tax profit	41

Balance Sheet at 31 December 199X

	(in £'000,000)
Fixed assets	175
Current assets	125
Total assets	300
Short-term liabilities	100
Long-term liabilities	155
Owners' equity	45
Total liabilities	300

people throughout the company. It was assumed that the people concerned would be grade two secretarial and clerical staff. Their salary would be in the range of £8,250 to £9,950 per annum.

It is generally assumed that the total staff cost is about 150% of the salary actually.

It was thought that 25% of these people would leave the firm due to the normal staff movement, about 25% could be used in other departments but that 50% of these individuals would have to be made redundant. The staff who would be made redundant would have to be paid on average about one year's salary as compensation. It was also believed that those members of staff who would remain in the sales office would need about one week's training each and should be given a salary increase of about 5%. The cost of the initial training was about £1,000 per person per week.

The production manager Karl Mann also felt that his operation might well be able to operate without as many clerks but this was not accurately quantified, although it was clear that there would be as many staff released as in the sales order processing functions. In general the production department faces the same cost parameters or profile as the sales office.

No requests have been forthcoming from any of the departments discussed above to prepare any redundancy papers. At the same time no recruiting has been done for any of the sales offices and it is assumed that those staff who would have normally been lost by natural wastage have probably gone. We have transferred about five people from these departments over the last few months.

By the way, the people we transferred out of the sales offices all said that they would be glad to get away from the new information system. It seems that it creates a lot of pressure for the staff working there.

Karl Mann was initially concerned that ISIS/2000 might meet with some resistance from his staff but this did not really happen. However a few of the people who have left the production department in the last year have said during their exit interview that the pressure of working with ISIS/2000, although not the main reason for leaving, was something they were looking forward to not having in their new jobs.

In conversation with the Sales Manager

An extract of a conversation with Frank O'Reilly, the Sales Manager of Proton Electronics Ltd.

The idea of the ISIS/2000, which is the first attempt that this firm ever had at an integrated sales order entry, inventory management, credit control, production scheduling and transport scheduling system, came from my division.

Our salesmen had been told by our clients and by our ex-clients that our competitors had already installed such systems. The computer systems which ISIS/2000 replaced in this firm, which were a number of separate mainframe systems, some work done on stand alone personal computers and other manual systems, had become so out of date that it was rather embarrassing.

We were just losing business to competitors who could deliver faster. If we hadn't modernised our systems we believed that we would have lost 2% to 3% of our turnover per year. In the first year that the system was in we stopped the flow of clients to our competitors and since then we have grown our sales at 2.5% per year and we expect that growth rate to double next year and double again the year after.

Of course we also hoped for efficiency and effectiveness improvements from ISIS/2000. Staff savings were discussed with the personnel department. It seems to me that we actually only achieved about 50% of these staff savings. Its implementation was more difficult than we had envisaged. There was at the outset a lot of hype from the sales people from ISIS Corporation, especially Fred Johnson. ISIS/2000 was 18 months late on being commissioned and cost nearly twice as much as the original estimate. We were surprised, or to be precise, Jerry King our Financial Director and Thomas Williamson the Chief Accountant were shocked by some of the hidden costs, or perhaps more accurately by some of the on-going costs, such as operations and maintenance.

With regards effectiveness, ISIS/2000 allows us to forecast our production requirements much more accurately. It helps us schedule our production in a much more sensible way.

It enables us to use our transport fleet in a way that has reduced our costs considerably.

On top of these cost savings our clients are much more satisfied with the service which we now offer. The right products are in the warehouse at the right time and we can now generally get the goods to the client within 24 hours of the order being received. This is worth a lot to us.

But in effect one of the major benefits of ISIS/2000 was to open our eyes to what can be achieved with IT in an organisation like ours. This system allowed us to stem a situation of competitive disadvantage. Now if we continue down the same logical path it will allow us to turn the tables on *our competitors and develop a significant competitive advantage. What we need is to introduce a comprehensive EDI system which will give us direct links to our major clients. This will transform the way we do business and will give us up to 10% growth per annum for some time.*

In conversation with the EDP Manager

An extract of a conversation with Joe Slithers, EDP Manager of Proton Electronics Ltd.

ISIS/2000 was estimated at costing £1.75 million for the hardware and about £350,000 for the software. In the event both budgets were overrun. The hardware cost £3.5 million and the software £2.1 million. Thus the cost was almost twice as much as planned. The commissioning costs were about £1.4 million. The on-going costs of the system are about £2.5 million per annum for all five offices. As the system has been in for three years we have spent about £7 million on ISIS/2000 so far. These figures are all based on marginal costs of the system.

The system was very troublesome in the first 12 months or so and put a lot of strain on this department. However after it was finally accepted and the staff training was completed its operation and maintenance has been very easy. Staff in the sales offices effectively do the whole thing themselves.

ISIS/2000 is a relatively small part of our IT expenditure. We spend nearly one per cent of our turnover per annum on our systems. For this sum of money we run two medium sized mainframes, several small minis and numerous personal computers. We also use outsourcers as we subcontract several systems to a local bureau. So far the outsourcing arrangements have been quite successful and despite my initial disquiet at the notion of outsourcing, as I thought that the IS staff might feel threatened by the presence of outsourcing, this has not happened, and in fact some of my people are very pleased with the new arrangements.

It must be remembered that Proton Electronics Ltd have always been very cautious with regards computing. George Edwards is a classic computerphobic and he covers this by insisting on a policy of scarce resources. We have to fight for every penny which is spent on information systems.

Of course, there are exceptions. Frank O'Reilly and that salesman from ISIS sold Edwards ISIS/2000 without him really understanding what was at issue and he then went overboard, not really understanding what was happening. The delays and overruns were due to the fact that the spec was not complete and that O'Reilly insisted that all the features of ISIS/2000 were real time. Background updating was simply not acceptable. So in order to deliver reasonable response times a huge amount of re-working of the code had to be done and extra fast processors and disk drives had to be purchased.

In a scarce resource culture little post implementation auditing is traditionally done. The argument which is usually given is that there are not enough people available to do them. In any case as funds are only released for projects which are desperately required, they will definitely show a good return. Of course we don't all believe this but a cultural change will be needed if any progress is to be made with regards these issues. And Thomas Williamson is just about as computerphobic as Edwards. When Gerry King retires, and I think that he has only a few months to go, there will be an opportunity to change a few things around here, maybe!

There is now talk about introducing EDI as well as a new generation of computer hardware and software which is referred to as ISIS/2020, but I am not at all sure that this makes much sense in a firm like Proton Electronics Ltd.

By the way although I welcome the appointment of a business systems development manager, I was not consulted about the creation of this post and I would be well pleased if someone would be so kind as to tell me what this role is actually expected to achieve.

In conversation with the Production Manager

An extract of a conversation with Karl Mann, Production Manager of Proton Electronics Ltd.

I was very sceptical about what ISIS/2000 could do for my department and of course when it was late and ran hopelessly over budget I felt entirely vindicated. I was also pretty sure that my staff would find it difficult to work with the system and that it would cause a lot more errors.

However, during the first year I began to see certain small improvements which actually began to grow and today I consider ISIS/2000 to be essential to the way we run our business. Instead of fulfilling my fears the staff actually took to the system very well, with one of our leading foremen acting as a systems champion within the factory environment. He has become so good at ensuring we get the most out of our systems that we are considering promoting him to management.

Besides the fact that I am able to do without replacing the six members of staff who left over the past three years I have been able to dramatically improve the use of our various manufacturing and processing facilities around the country. We are able to forecast the demand for various products much better than we could before. We are able to have much longer runs for certain products. We can better control machine downtime by using our utilisation reports and scheduling preventative maintenance instead of only fire fighting when things went wrong.

As a result of the above I have been able to reduce our inventories of raw material as well as our work-in-progress and also our finished goods. I estimate that we have reduced the salary bill by about £150,000 per annum in this department alone. We have reduced the various inventories by about £2.5 million and have also improved factory utilisation by about 5%.

I am also responsible for the firm's transportation fleet of about 50 trucks in all. They are now on the road 10% more and get their payloads to our clients much faster by better routing. Our transport costs are down by at least 4%.

But one of the most important benefits which the system has delivered is the reduction in errors. We used to get a lot of errors due to mis-calculations, bits of paper getting lost, goods being sent to the wrong address, etc. These have almost been eliminated. There is a much more positive attitude amongst my team who could not really function without ISIS/2000.

Of course we are now really looking forward to Frank O'Reilly's new suggestion as we believe EDI is the way forward for us. However, I know that this won't be easy to sell to the managing director who really has not looked kindly on any of our efforts to computerise the firm.

In conversation with the Financial Director

An extract of a conversation with Gerry King, Financial Director of Proton Electronics Ltd.

I joined Proton Electronic in the very early days, just a few months after George Edwards was promoted to Managing Director. George had previously been the chief accountant here and when his predecessor suddenly died he found himself at the helm. The organisation was no where near as solid then as it is today and all credit for that must go to George Edwards. He has always kept a very tight ship and he very skilfully uses financial controls to make sure that he realises his targets.

His main problem with computing is that it is so expensive and that it seems very hard to keep to budgets and deadlines. This produces a very negative reaction in George Edwards and he can then become fairly negative towards the people and the issues involved. This has sort of happened with ISIS/2000. However I am sure that if you can demonstrate the benefits which we have obtained from this system in clear financial terms you will find that his attitude will change.

Anyway I am retiring in a few weeks. You don't happen to be a Chartered Accountant by any chance?

In conversation with Fred Johnson, Salesman, ISIS Corporation

I am sure that you will have heard from several members of Protons staff that the organisation's information systems already needs upgrading and that we are proposing a new platform which we call ISIS/2020.

ISIS/2020 has very much more to offer Proton Electronics Limited. It is a state of the art leading edge approach to electronic commerce through a number of Internet and Web enabled inter organisational systems (IOS) with the main focus on electronic data interchange. ISIS/2020 is in fact the most powerful system of its generation on the market and it is just what Proton Electronics Limited needs to close the competitive gap which has been opening up between itself and some of the market leaders in the past few years. This is despite the good things which have been achieved by ISIS/2000. The delays produced in commissioning this system actually set Proton back more than they generally realise.

Of course, as every one knows power and complexity go hand in hand and thus considerably more care will be needed in how Proton Electronics Limited implements ISIS/2020.

We have not quite finalised our proposal to the board of directors as the Managing Director, George Edwards insisted that your review of the situation should be taken into account before they will make the final decision.

However in general ISIS/2020 will require a new hardware platform which will cost the organisation about £4 million. This number could actually vary and in the end it could be as much as £5 million if they go for the full range of options. The systems software cost will be £750,000 but the application software is also quite variable and we envisage the range of cost being between £3 million and £4 million. There will be communications set up costs of £500,000.

ISIS/2020 will involve quite a lot of reorganisation as well as changes to working practices, and thus the commissioning cost should be budgeted at between £1 and £1.5 million. Retraining will also be needed and this will cost between £250,000 and £400,000.

The benefits identification programme has not yet been finally concluded. But current indications suggest that in the first year of operation ISIS/2020 should generate somewhere between £4 and £5 million in revenue improvement. In addition there should be about £900,000 in cost reduction of overheads. It is thought that these benefits will grow year by year as the organisation moves up the learning curve. A conservative estimate suggests that there will be annual improvements in both revenue production and cost reduction of 15% while there are those in the organisation who believe that these improvements will actually be 20%.

Proton Electronics Limited's cost of capital has been over the past 10 years somewhere between 15% and 25%. The financial director normally uses 20% as an average whenever Proton needs to use this figure in a calculation.

Of course we are aware that the ISIS/2020 project is not risk free for Proton Electronics Limited but on the other hand if they do nothing then the competitive gap will just widen and their business is gracefully degraded until they are actually out of business.

ISIS/2020 should be viable for five to seven years and return to Proton Electronics Limited the market position it had some years ago.

Petra Jones appears to us to be the leader which Proton Electronics Limited needs to be able to make a leading edge project like ISIS/2020 really work. Proton Electronics Limited should really take every opportunity to advance this project immediately as the sooner they begin the sooner the benefits will start to flow.

Appendix A

Business case development questionnaires and forms

BUSINESS OUTCOME DETAILS

Project:	Stage:
Document No:	Date:
Author:	

Macro Model

Macro model	Details
Name of the proposed intervention *Limit this to around 10 words*	
State the perceived problem or opportunity *Limit this to around 100 words*	
Why is it a problem or opportunity? *Limit this to around 75 words*	
What is the nature of the intervention? *Limit this to around 50 words*	
What will be the result of the intervention? *Limit this to around 75 words*	
Identify the owner-users *List up to five possible owners/users of the intervention*	

Meso model

Business Output	Business Outcome	Specific Benefits	Measurement Method	Specific Metric	Responsibility

Business outcome details

Micro Model

Using IT to automate jobs	All costs in 000's			
Cost displacement	Year 0	Year 1	Year 2	Year 3
Set up costs				
Hardware including PCs, LANs and other peripherals				
Software including spreadsheet, WP, database and comms				
Training				
Installation and testing				
Total initial cost				
Monthly on-going costs				
Staffing, including support				
Maintenance & upgrades				
General				
Total costs				
Monthly benefits				
Reduction in clerical salaries				
Reduction in supervisory salaries				
Reduction in other staff costs				
Office space released				
Other office expenses saved				
Total benefits				
Improvement per month				
Annual net benefit				
Simple annual ROI				
Simple payback				
Cost of capital				
Discounted annual net benefit				
Discounted payback				
Net present value				
Internal rate of return				
Profitability index				

STAKEHOLDERS DETAILS

Project:	Stage:
Document No:	Date:
Author:	

Stakeholder check list

Key questions	Details
Who has most to gain from the project's success and failure?	
What capacity does each stakeholder have to help or hinder the project?	
Whose attitude do you most want to change and why?	
Which stakeholder should you most concentrate your efforts on?	
Who is the project sponsor?	
Who is the project champion?	
Who is the project's main adversary?	
What action are you going to take with respect to each of the key stakeholders?	

STRATEGY

Project:		Stage:	
Document No:		Date:	
Author:			

Corporate strategy

	Strategic model	Details
1.1	What is the corporate strategy? *Limit this to around 50 words*	

Strategic alignment using the generic strategy model

Function	Low cost	Differentiation

Strategic alignment using the value discipline model

Function	Best product	Best total cost	Best total solution

TECHNOLOGY

Project:	Stage:
Document No:	Date:
Author:	

Technology review

Issue	Current assessment
Is the proposed project technically doable?	
Does the proposed technology conform to the organisation's IT architecture?	
Should all or part of the project be outsourced?	
What would be the primary advantage of outsourcing this project?	
Are there any possible bottlenecks or obstacles, which could prevent delivery?	
Does the organisation have the IT competencies to deliver?	
Can the IT team produce the required deliverables in an appropriate time scale?	
What issues could cause material delays to the proposed timetable for this project?	
Does the project budget look reasonable?	
What aspects of the budget are the most exposed to over-runs?	
Is the organisation capable of absorbing the implications of the proposed system?	
Is there any other compelling reason why the project should not be undertaken?	

Cost benefit analysis

Cost Displacement – One Year

Using IT to automate jobs	All costs in 000s		
Cost displacement	Year 0	Year 1	
Set up costs			
Hardware including PCs, LANs and other peripherals			
Software including s'sheet, WP, database and coms			
Training			
Installation & testing			
Total			
Monthly on-going costs			
Staffing, including support			
Maintenance & upgrades			
General			
Total			
Monthly benefits			
Reduction in clerical salaries			
Reduction in supervisory salaries			
Reduction in other staff costs			
Office space released			
Other office expenses saved			
Total			
Improvement per month			
Annual net benefit			
Annual ROI			
Simple payback			Years

Cost displacement – Three Years

Using IT to automate jobs	All costs in 000's			
Cost displacement	Year 0	Year 1	Year 2	Year 3
Set up costs				
Hardware including PCs, LANs and other peripherals				
Software including spreadsheet, WP, database and comms				
Training				
Installation and testing				
Total initial cost				
Monthly on-going costs				
Staffing, including support				
Maintenance & upgrades				
General				
Total costs				
Monthly benefits				
Reduction in clerical salaries				
Reduction in supervisory salaries				
Reduction in other staff costs				
Office space released				
Other office expenses saved				
Total benefits				
Improvement per month				
Annual net benefit				
Simple annual ROI				
Simple payback				
Cost of capital				
Discounted annual net benefit				
Discounted payback				
Net present value				
Internal rate of return				
Profitability index				

Cost Displacement – Five Years

Using IT to automate jobs	All costs in 000's					
Cost displacement	Yr 0	Yr 1	Yr 2	Yr 3	Yr 4	Yr 5
Set up costs						
Hardware including PCs, LANs and other peripherals						
Software including s'sheet, WP, database and coms						
Training						
Installation & testing						
Total initial costs						
Monthly on-going costs						
Staffing, including support						
Maintenance & upgrades						
General						
Total costs						
Monthly benefits						
Reduction in clerical salaries						
Reduction in supervisory salaries						
Reduction in other staff costs						
Office space released						
Other office expenses saved						
Total benefits						
Net improvement per month						
Annual net benefit						
Simple annual ROI						
Simple payback						
Cost of capital						
Discounted Annual Net Benefit						
Discounted payback						
Net Present Value						
Internal Rate of Return						
Profitability Index						

Cost Avoidance – Five Years

Using IT to automate jobs	All costs in 000's					
Cost avoidance	Year 0	Year 1	Year 2	Year 3	Year 4	Year 5
Set up costs						
Hardware						
Software						
Training						
Installation & testing						
Total						
Monthly on-going costs						
Staffing, including support						
Maintenance & upgrades						
General						
Total						
Monthly benefits						
Staff no required						
Other costs avoided						
Total						
Improvement per month						
Annual net benefit						
Annual ROI						
Simple payback						
Cost of capital						
Discounted annual net benefit						
Net present value						
Internal rate of return						
Profitability index						

Cost benefit analysis

Decision Analysis–Five Years

Using IT to improve performance through more information	All costs in 000s					
Decision analysis	Year 0	Year 1	Year 2	Year 3	Year 4	Year 5
Set up costs						
Hardware						
Software						
Initial training						
Commissioning						
Installation & testing						
Total						
Monthly on-going costs						
Staffing, including Support						
On-going training						
Maintenance & upgrades						
General						
Total						
Monthly benefits						
Reduction in bad debts						
Interest earned by faster receipts						
Reduction in obsolete inventories						
Increased sales due to better availability						
Total						
Improvement per month						
Annual net benefit						
Annual ROI						
Simple payback						
Cost of capital						
Discounted annual net benefit						
Net present value						
Internal rate of return						
Profitability index						

Time Release Improvement

Using IT to improve salesperson's productivity		
Investment costs for 10 systems	All costs in 000s	
Set up costs		
PCs, cellular modems and peripherals		
Database, spreadsheet, WP and communications		
Training		
Installation and testing		
Total initial cost		
Monthly on-going costs		
Staffing, including Support		
Communications costs		
Maintenance		
General		
Amortisation		
Total monthly cost		
Monthly benefit analysis		
Average no. of sales calls per day		
Average value of sales per call		
Reduction in average sales call time		
Reduction in time required for daily form filling		
Total time release		
Average travel time required between sales calls		
Average additional opportunity as a result of IT investment		
Monthly revenue analysis		
Resulting additional revenue		
Profit margin %		
Daily profit improvement from 10 systems		
Monthly profit improvement per salesperson (22 days per month)		
Monthly profit improvement from 10 systems		
Annual profit improvement		
Annual operating cost of system		
Annual net benefit		
ROI		
Payback		Years

Cost benefit analysis

Transformation Project A (7)

Using IT to improve performance through more information					
Transformation project		All costs in 000s			
Set up costs	Year 0	Year 1	Year 2	Year 3	Year 4
Hardware					
Software					
Reorganisation costs					
Initial training					
Commissioning					
Total initial costs					
Annual on-Going IT costs of project					
Staff					
Maintenance					
General					
Amortisation					
Total on-going costs					
Annual benefits		Year 1	Year 2	Year 3	Year 4
Additional sales					
Cost of sales					
Net profit					
Tax					
After tax profit					
Amortisation					
Net cash flow					
Cost of capital					
Tax rate					
Economic life of the project in years					
Net present value					
Internal rate of return					
Profitability index					

Transformation Project B (8)

Using IT to improve performance through more information					
Transformation project		All costs in 000s			
Set up costs	Year 0	Year 1	Year 2	Year 3	Year 4
Hardware					
Software					
Reorganisation costs					
Training					
Commissioning					
Total project costs					
Annual on-going it costs					
Staff					
Maintenance					
General					
Amortisation					
Total costs					
Annual benefits		Year 1	Year 2	Year 3	Year 4
Additional sales					
Cost of Sales					
Net profit					
Tax					
After tax profit					
Amortisation					
Cash flow					
Investment cash flow					
Net cash flow					
Cost of capital					
Tax rate					
Economic life of the project					
Net present value					
Internal rate of return					
Profitability index					

Evaluating a business case

Project:	Stage:
Document No:	Date:
Author:	

Evaluation form

Consider each of the five factors in the figure below and weight them in their relative importance on a scale of 1 = least important and 5 = most important.

Review each project, one at a time, and ascertain how well each project performs on each of the five factors. Use a scoring system between 1 and 10 where 1= very poor and 10 = excellent.

Multiply the weights by the scores for each factor and then add the resultant values. The project with the highest total value should, all other things being equal, be the project with the best business case and thus the most suitable project.

Issue	Project 1			Project 2			Project 3		
	Wt.	Sc.	Value	Wt.	Sc.	Value	Wt.	Sc.	Value
Business and finance understanding									
Stakeholder commitment									
Strategic alignment									
Technology competence									
Risk									
Total									

(Wt = Weight and Sc = Score)

Appendix B

Financial measures used in cost-benefit analysis

Payback

The payback may be defined as the amount of time, usually expressed in years and months, required for the original investment amount to be repaid by the cash-in flows. This measure is sometimes used with nominal cash-in flows and sometimes used with discounted cash-in flows. Nominal cash flows are the amounts unadjusted for the time value of money. The most popular form of payback used today is referred to as the exhaust method. The exhaust method of payback calculation involves the deduction of each year's cash-in flow from the original investment until the original amount is reduced to zero. This method should be contrasted with the average payback method which only gives a rough approximation of the period of time required to recover the investment amount when the cash-in flows are relatively constant.

Exhaust method

Payback in time (years,months,etc) = Investment – Cumulative benefit

The calculation of the payback by the exhaust method is a reiterative process which requires the cumulative benefit to be subtracted from the investment until the result is zero. The time at which the result is zero represents the period which is required for the investment amount to be returned.

Average method

Payback in time $\quad = \dfrac{\text{Investment}}{\text{Average annual benefit}}$

This average method is only useful if the annual benefits do not materially vary from the average. If there is any substantial variability in the annual benefits this method will produce meaningless results. Many firms use the payback as the primary criterion for deciding whether an investment is suitable or not.

It is generally considered that the cash flows used to calculate the payback should have first been discounted. This is referred to as a discounted payback. If this is done it will produce a time-value-based payback measure which will reflect the cost of capital. A discounted payback will always show a longer period than one based on nominal values.

Net present value (NPV)

The net present value may be defined as the difference between the sum of the values of the cash-in flows, discounted at an appropriate cost of capital, and the present value of the original investment. Provided the NPV is greater than or equal to zero the investment will earn the firm's required rate of return. The size of the NPV may be considered as either a measure of the surplus which the investment makes over its required return, or as a margin of error in the size of the investment amount.

Present value of benefit $\quad = \dfrac{\text{Benefit}}{(1+i)^n}$

Where $\quad i$ = rate of interest
$\quad\quad\quad\quad n$ = number of years

NPV = $\sum$ Present value of benefit – Present value of investment

The interpretation of the NPV should be based on the rules:

If NPV $\geq$ 0 then invest
If NPV $<$ 0 then do not invest

The size of the NPV represents the margin of error which may be made in the estimate of the investment amount before the investment will be rejected.

Profitability index (PI)

The profitability index is defined as the sum of the present values of the cash-in flows divided by the present value of the investment. This shows a rate of return expressed as the number of discounted pounds and pence which the investment will earn for every pound originally invested.

$$PI = \frac{\sum \text{Present value of benefits}}{\text{Present value of investment}}$$

Internal rate of return (IRR)

The internal rate of return is the rate of interest which will cause the NPV to be zero. It is the internally generated return which the investment will earn throughout its life. It is also frequently referred to as the yield of the investment.

$$IRR = i \text{ such that } NPV = 0$$

Rate of return or return on investment (ROI)

The rate of return or return on investment, which is sometimes referred to as the simple return on investment, is calculated by considering the annual benefit divided by the investment amount. Sometimes an average rate of return for the whole period of investment is calculated by averaging the annual benefits while on other occasions the rate of return is calculated on a year by year basis using individual benefit amounts.

$$ROI = \frac{\text{Annual benefit}}{\text{Investment amount}}$$

Appendix C

Glossary of terms

Automate

IT systems that are developed to replace manual activities are referred to as automate systems.

Benefit

A term used to indicate an advantage, profit or gain attained by an individual or organisation. A benefit is normally traded-off against a cost of some sort.

Business objectives

Those objectives a business organisation wishes to achieve. In the context of this book, the organisational changes and improvements that are to be achieved in order to enhance the business performance as a result of the information system's development and commissioning.

Business value

Something of worth to the organisation. Business value refers to how much the information system contributes to the overall worth of the business. This does not simply refer to short-term cost improvements but to a full range of issues including both hard and soft benefits q.v.

Business vision

The business vision is that which the management wants to achieve with the enterprise in the future. A business vision usually refers to the medium to long term. It is often expressed in terms of a series of specific objectives as well as general values.

Capital investment

Funds committed to long-term assets within the firm such as land and building, plant and equipment or computer hardware. In some cases computer software is even regarded as a capital investment.

Co-creation

A co-creation approach means that all the stakeholders' interests are considered in deciding how to specify the proposed information system at the outset.

Co-evolutionary

A co-evolutionary approach means that all the stakeholders' interests are considered in deciding how to proceed with an information system's development. This needs to be contrasted with either the information systems people deciding what the eventual user needs and producing an information system for them, or the user demanding an information system without understanding what is possible or desirable from the different points of view of the other stakeholders.

Competitive advantage

This term is usually used to describe how one particular organisation attracts clients or customers when in competition with another. There are various sources of competitive advantage including low cost and differentiation.

Contingency

The contingency notion or concept states that it is not possible to be fully knowledgeable of the precise outcomes required from an information system at the outset of its development. As a result of this uncertainty information systems developers' plan can only be contingent on the current assumptions not changing. Once an assumption changes the development plan will need to reflect this change.

Corporate memory

The ability of the organisation to recall useful information about techniques and procedures required to conduct its business. The term is sometimes associated with the notion of empowering staff to perform tasks requiring greater skills than they would otherwise be able to undertake.

Corporate strategy

A method through which the firm finds, gets and keeps its clients. In a broad sense it refers to how the firm relates to and interacts with its environment, including its stakeholders.

Cost avoidance

A technique used in cost-benefit analysis which attempts to measure the various costs which an organisation will not have to incur when it acquires an information system.

Cost-benefit analysis (CBA)

The process of comparing the various costs associated with an investment with the benefits and the profits which it generates. Cost-benefit analysis attempts to demonstrate whether the investment will earn a sufficient return in order for the organisation to consider it to be economically worth-while. There are a number of different approaches to cost-benefit analysis including cost displacement, cost avoidance, risk analysis, etc.

Cost displacement

A technique used in cost-benefit analysis which attempts to measure the various costs to which an organisation will no longer be committed when it acquires an information system. The new information system will be the cost and the benefits will be the expenses which the firm will no longer have to incur.

Critical success factors (CSF)

Those aspects of the business which must be right for the enterprise to succeed in achieving its objectives. It is also sometimes said that even though all other aspects of the business are going well, if the critical success factors are not being achieved, then the business will not succeed.

Culture gap

Term to describe the high degree of misunderstanding and sometimes animosity between management and information systems groups.

Decision analysis

A technique used in cost-benefit analysis which attempts to measure the impact of information systems on decisions made by individuals in the firm. Decision analysis is based on the proposition that better information can lead to better decisions which in turn can lead to better financial results.

Deliverables

The demonstrable results of a system or an initiative.

Direct cost

The cost incurred which may be shown as being incurred specifically due to some activity or project and not simply associated with the general overheads of the business. Direct costs vary in some proportion to the level of output.

Evaluation

In general terms, evaluation can be described as the determination of the worth or value of something judged according to appropriate criteria.

Ex-ante

Refers to estimates of the benefits and the costs in advance of an investment.

Ex-post

Refers to the actual cost and estimates of the achieved benefits after the implementation of the investment.

Feedback loop

In the context of this book, the last part of the evaluation cycle in which documents are used as input to the next formative evaluation session to ensure that the business, financial and project pictures are not out of date or out of touch with the actual current requirements.

Formative evaluation

Formative evaluation is an iterative evaluation and decision, making process continually influencing decisions about the information system's development process and the resulting information system. The term 'formative evaluation' has its origins in the evaluation of educational programmes and social programmes (Scriven 1991; Patton 1980). The phenomenon of formative evaluation is not new (Chelimsky 1997). It has been applied for many years in a number of disciplines with the roots of the concept stretching back into the nineteenth century. The word formative derives from to 'mould by discipline and education' (Shorter Oxford Dictionary, 1983). This is very close to the approach used by Walsham (1993) which he refers to as interpretative evaluation and which he highlights as an important facet in information systems management. This is also sometimes termed 'learning evaluation'.

Framework

It is a fundamental structure for a system of ideas where a structure is a number of parts that are put together in a particular way.

Generic strategy

One of the basic ways in which a firm can find, get and keep its clients. According to Porter (1985) there are two generic strategies, which are cost leadership and differentiation. A generic strategy may be broad based or focused on a niche in the market.

Hard cost

Costs associated with an investment that are agreed by everyone to be directly attributable to the investment, and which can be easily captured by accounting procedures.

Hidden cost

A non-obvious cost associated with an investment that may in fact appear to be due to another source.

Informate

IT systems that provide specific information to management, which allow them to make more insightful decisions and therefore use the organisation's resources more effectively, are referred to as informate systems.

Intangible benefit

Benefits produced by an investment which are not immediately obvious and/or measurable in financial terms.

IT benefit

The benefit produced by an investment in information technology. It is likely that such an investment will produce both tangible and intangible IT benefits.

IT business benefits

This normally refers to advantages, profits or gains which are delivered by the use of information systems. This traditionally involves performing tasks faster, with fewer errors and producing higher quality output than could otherwise be achieved.

Macro model

A high level model employing general concepts, or rough drawings, or imprecise fabrications to present a conceptual picture which will contextualise the problem or opportunity as well as provide a suggested solution.

Marginal cost

The cost associated with the production of one extra unit or the cost involved in a new activity excluding the general overhead.

Meso model

Adds some detail to a macro model, but will still be expressed primarily in generalities.

Micro model

A detailed model which attempts to be closer to reality and thus to use more specific or life-like representations or values.

Model

A representation of an artefact, a construction, a system or an event or sequence of events.

NPV (net present value)

The difference between the sum of the values of the cash inflows, discounted at an appropriate cost of capital, and the present value of the original investment. Provided the NPV is greater than or equal to zero the investment will earn the firm's required rate of return.

Opportunity cost

The opportunity cost of an investment is the amount which the organisation could have earned if the sum invested in IT was used in another way.

Outcome

In the context of this book, the business result of the information system after it has been successfully commissioned and implemented.

Overhead cost

The overhead costs are the costs of running the business which do not vary directly with the level of output. Overhead costs tend to increase in step functions i.e. the increases are of relatively large amounts associated with such activities as acquiring an additional factory, etc.

Outcome space

Term used to describe the business benefits of an information system.

Payback

The amount of time, usually expressed in years and months, required for an original investment to be repaid by the cash inflows.

Process

In the context of this book a process can be defined as a series of structured activities which are started at project initialisation and continue until project termination.

Risk

The possibility that the actual input variables and the outcomes may vary from those originally estimated.

Risk analysis

A technique used to assess the potential profitability of an investment. It involves the use of ranges as input variables rather than single point estimates. Probabilities may be associated with these ranges. The output of risk analysis is a profile of a series of possible results.

ROI (return on investment)

Accounting or financial management term to describe how well the firm has used its resources. It is usually calculated by dividing net profit after tax by total net assets.

Scope creep

The tendency for information systems projects to expand in order to embrace a wider range of issues than originally intended.

SDLC (software development life cycle)

The traditional approach to information systems development.

Soft cost

Costs associated with an investment that are not readily agreed by everyone to be directly attributable to the investment, and which are not easily captured by accounting procedures.

Stakeholder

Any individual with an involvement in the evaluation process. Can include senior management, users, financial managers, technical staff, etc.

Strategic alignment

In the context of this book, strategic alignment refers to ensuring that the information systems effort of the organisation supports the overall corporate strategy.

Strategic evaluation

A necessary preparatory activity to strategic decision making at agreed milestones in the development cycle.

Strategic information system (SIS)

An information system which helps a firm improve its long-term performance by achieving its corporate strategy and thereby directly increasing its contribution to the industry value chain.

Strategic vision

How the top management of an enterprise believes it can achieve its objectives in the medium- to long-term.

Strategy

The formal use of this word refers to the way a firm finds, gets and keeps its clients. Common usage has reduced the meaning of strategy to be synonymous with plan. See also 'corporate strategy' and 'generic strategy'.

Summative evaluation

According to Finne et al. (1995) summative evaluation approaches typically aim at assessing outcomes and impacts; they take place towards the end of the programme or after its conclusion. They go on to point out that summative evaluations may be used conceptually, instrumentally, or persuasively. This means that the results of such an evaluation may be used to reconsider an investment proposal, to redirect investment efforts or to convince others that a new course of action is required.

Tangible benefit

Benefits produced by investments that are immediately obvious and measurable. The term tangible benefit is usually used to refer to benefits that are directly reflected in the improvement in the profit performance of the organisation.

Transformate

IT systems that make a radical impact on the way in which the organisation conducts its business, either by the transformation of its current activities and processes, or by the introduction of new lines of business are referred to as transformate systems.

Vision

Sometimes referred to as 'strategic vision' or 'business vision' q.v., this term refers to a view as to how the firm can successfully function in the marketplace in the medium- to long-term. It usually encompasses how the firm will find, get and keep its clients.

Appendix D

References and bibliography

Adams D, 1982, *Life, the universe and everything*, Seventh printing, p33, Pan Books Limited, London.

Adelman C, 1996, "Anything Goes: Evaluation and Relativism", *Evaluation*, Vol. 2, No 3, pp 291-305.

Akkermans H, 1995, "Developing a logistic strategy through participative business modelling", *International Journal of Operations and Production Management*, p100-112, Vol 15, Issue 11.

Ansoff H I, 1965: *Corportate Strategy*, Penguin, London.

Benjamin R I, De Long and Scott-Morton, M S, 1990, "Electronic Data Interchange: How Much Competitive Advantage?", A collection of papers entitled *Planning for Information as a Corporate Resource: The Best of Long Range Planning*, No. 4 Pergamon Press, Oxford.

Bernstein P, 1996, *Against the Gods*, p7, John Wiley and Sons, New York.

Boyadjian S, and Warren O, 1987, Cited in RISKS, *Reading Corporate Signals*, John Wiley and Sons Ltd, Chichester.

Bradley K, 1996, *PRINCE - A Practical Handbook*, p129, Butterworth Heinemann, Oxford.

Brunner. I. and Guzman. A, 1989. "Participatory Evaluation: A Tool to Assess Projects and Empower People". In Conner. R. F. and Hendricks. M. (Eds). *International Innovations in Evaluation Methodology: New Directions for Evaluation Methodology*. Jossey-Bass, San Francisco, CA.

Cane A, 1992, "The number crunchers crack", *Financial Times*, June 7th.

Chandler A, 1990, *Strategy and Structure: Chapters in the History of the American Industrial Enterprise*, p13, MIT Press, Boston, Mass.

Chapman C, and Ward S, 1997, *Project Risk Management – Processes, Techniques and Insights.* John Wiley and Sons. Chichester.

Chelimsky E, 1997, "The Coming Transformations in Evaluation", in E. Chelimsky and W. R. Shadish eds *Evaluation for the 21st Century,* Sage Publications, London.

Corbitt T, 1995, Business modelling techniques, *Management Services*, p 22-23, Vol 38, Issue 5, May.

Correia C, 1989, *Financial Management,* Second edition, Juta & Co., Ltd, Cape Town.

Disraeli B, 1959, cited in *Mark Twain, Autobiography,* ch. 29, ed.Neider C.

Drucker P, 1997, What Executives Need to Learn, cited by Davenport T, in *Information Ecology – Mastering the information and knowledge environment,* Oxford University Press, New York.

Earl M, 1992, Putting IT in its place: a polemic for the nineties, *Journal of Information systems,* September, vol 7, no 3, p 100.

Economist, 1991 ,"Too many computers spoil the broth", p 30, 24 August.

Fairley R, 1990, "Risk Management: The key to successful software projects", in *Experiences with the management of software projects,* Workshop Series, No 9.

Farbey B, Land F, Targett D, 1993, *How to Assess your IT Investment- A study of methods and practice,* Butterworth Heinemann, p41, Oxford.

Finne H, Levin M & Nilssen T, 1995, Trailing Research: A Model for Useful Program Evaluation, *Evaluation* Vol. 1, No 1, July Sage Publications, London, UK.

Fortune J and Peters G, 1995, *Learning from Failure – the Systems Approach,* John WIley and Sons, Chichester.

Loveman G, *Computerworld,* November 25, 1991, quoted in Tom Peters, *Liberation Management,* p 125, Alfred A Knopf, New York.

Gonin R and Money A H, 1990, *Nonlinear L_p - norm Estimation,* Marcel Dekker

Gould, S J., 1992, *The Mismeasure of Man,* P27, Penguin Books,London.

Hewett T T, 1986, "The Role of Iterative Evaluation in Designing Systems Usability". *Proceedings of 2nd. BCS HCI Specialist Group Conference, People and Computers: Designing for Usability*, Harrison M D and Monk D (eds.), York.

Hitt L and Brynjolfsson E, 1994, "The Three Faces of IT Value: Theory and Evidence", *Proceedings of the Fifteenth International Conference on Information Systems*. ICIS, Vancouver, British Columbia, Canada, December 14-17.

Hochstrasser B and Griffiths, C, 1990, *"Regaining Control of IT Investments"*, Kobler Unit, Imperial College, London.

Hopwood A G, 1983, "Evaluating the Real Benefits", in *New Office Technology, Human and Organisational Aspect*, Otway H J and Peltu M (eds.), Pinter Ltd., London.

Johnson N L and Kotz S, 1970 *Distributions in Statistics: Continuous Univariate Distributions*, Volumes 1 and 2, Houghton Mifflin.

Karlin S,1982, *11*th R.A. Fisher Memorial Lecture, Royal Society, London, April 20.

Kay J, 1993, *Foundations of Corporate Success*, Oxford University Press, Oxford.

Keen P, 1991, *Shaping the future - Business design through Information technology*, Harvard Business School Press, Boston, pp142.

Keynes J M, 1923, *A Tract on Monetary Reform*, ch. 3., cited in *Columbia Dictionary of Quotations*, Columbia University Press, Columbia.

Keynes J M, 1953, *The General Theory of Employment, Interest and Money* (first published in 1936), Harcourt Brace Jovanivich, Orlando.

Koella J, 1991, "On the use of mathematical models of malaria transmission", *Acta* 49, p2.

Lacity M, and Hirschheim R, 1995, *Information systems outsourcing*, John Wiley and Sons, Chichester.

Laudon K, 1989, *A General Model for Understanding the Relationship between Information Technology and Organizations*, New York University, Center for Research on Information Systems, New York, January.

Lincoln T, 1986, "Do Computer Systems Really Pay-off?", *Information and Management*, vol. 11.

Love A J, 1991, Internal Evaluation: Building Organisations from Within", *Applied Social Research Methods Series*, Vol. 24, Sage Publications.

Lyytinen K, 1987, "Expectation Failure Concept and Systems Analysts' View of Information Systems failures: Results of an Exploratory Study", *Information & Management*, Vol. 14, pp 45-46.

Mayne J and Zapio-Goni E, eds, 1997, *Monitoring Performance in the Public Sector: Future Directions from International Experience*, Transaction Publishers, New Brunswick and London.

McFarlan F W, 1990, A video produced on the subject of information management, Harvard Business School.

McFarlan F W, 1994, "Information Technology changes the way you compete", *Harvard Business Review*, May - June.

Oz E, 1994, "Informations Systems MIS-Development: The Case of Star* Doc", *Journal of Systems Management*, September.

Pascale R, 1986, *The Art of Japanese Management*, Penguin Books, p80.

Patton M Q, 1980, *Qualitative Evaluation Methods*, Sage Publications Inc., Beverly Hills, California, 1980.

Picciotto R, 1999, Towards an Economics of Evaluation, *Evaluation*, Vol 5, No. 3: 7-22

Porter M E, 1985, *Competitive Advantage – Creating and Sustaining Superior Performance*, The Free Press, New York.

Porter M E,1985, *Competitive Strategy - Techniques for Analysing Industries and Competitors*, The Free Press, New York.

Proctor T, 1995, Business Modelling on a personal computer, *Management Decision*, p38-43, Vol 33, Issue 9, 1995.

Quinn J B, 1988, cited in Quinn J B, Mintzberg H, James, R. M. (eds) *The Strategic Process, Concepts, Contexts and Cases*, Prentice Hall, New York.

Remenyi D S J, Money A. and Twite A, 1993, *A Guide to Measuring and Managing IT Benefits*, Second Edition, NCC Blackwell, Oxford.

Remenyi D, Money A. and Twite A, 1995, *Effective Measurement and Management of IT Costs and Benefits*, Butterworth-Heinemann, Oxford.

Remenyi D, Sherwood-Smith M and White T, 1997, *Achieving Maximum Benefit from your IS Investment*, John Wiley and Son, Chichester.

Remenyi D, 1999, *Stop IT Project Faliures Through Risk Management*, Butterworth-Heinemann, Oxford.

Romtech Report, 1989, *Computing Opinion Survey*, survey conducted by Romtech.

Russell B, 1925, *The ABC of Relativity*, Mentor Books, New American Library, by arrangement with George Allen and Unwin, 1960 p.144

Scriven M S, 1991, "The Science of Valuing", in *Foundations of Program Evaluation: Theories and Practice*, by Shadish W R *et al*, Sage Publications, Newbury Park, CA.

Senge P, 1992, *The Fifth Discipline - The Art and Practice of the Learning Organisation*, Random House Sydney, Australia.

Shadish W R, Cook T D and Leviton LC, 1991, *Foundations of program evaluation: Theories of Practice*, Sage Publications, Newbury Park, CA.

Sherwood-Smith M H, 1989, *The Evaluation of Computer-Based Office Systems*. Ph.D. unpublished thesis. University College Dublin.

Stalk G and Hout T, 1990, *Competing Against Time*, The Free Press, New York.

Strassmann, P. A., 1996, *Information Payoff: The Transformation of Work in the Electronic Age*, Free Press, New York.

Strassmann P, 1997, *The Squandered Computer: Evaluating the Business Alignment of Information Technologies*, Information Economics Press, New Canaan, Connecticut.

Svendsen A, 1998, *The Stakeholders Strategy*, Berrett-Koehler, San Francisco.

Symons V, 1991, A review of information systems evaluation: Content, Context and Process, *European Journal of Information Systems*, vol 1, no 3 pp 205-212.

Treacy M and Wiersema F, 1993, "Customer intimacy and other value disciplines", *Harvard Business Review*", p84-93, Jan-Feb.

Turner J R, 1995, *The Commercial Project Manager*, McGraw Hill, Maidenhead.

Walsham G, 1993, *Interpreting Information Systems In organisations*, Wiley, Chichester.

Wheatley M, 1992, *Leadership and the New Science*, p8, Berrett-Koeler Publishers, San Francisco.

Wiersema F, 1996, *Customer Intimacy*, p 31, Knowledge Exchange, Santa Monica, CA.

Willcocks L, 1991, *Unpublished Chairman's Introduction to a Conference on Managing IT Investment*, conducted by Business Intelligence, London 20 May.

Willcocks L and Griffiths C, 1994, *Beyond 2000: The Source Book for Major Projects*, The Major Projects Society, Templeton College, Oxford.

Zelm M, Vernadat F and Kosanke K, 1995, "The CIMOSA business modelling process", *Computers in Industry*, p 123-142, Vol, 26, Issue 2, Oct.

Zuboff S, 1998, *In the Age of the Smart Machine: The Future of Work and Power*, Basic Books, New York.

Index